Mary Among Us

The Apparitions at Oliveto Citra

ROBERT FARICY, S.J.
LUCIANA PECORAIO

Mary Among Us
The Apparitions at Oliveto Citra

Franciscan University Press
Franciscan University of Steubenville
Steubenville, OH 43952

DECLARATION

The decree of the Congregation for the Propagation of the Faith, A.A.S. 58, 1186 (approved by Pope Paul VI on October 14, 1966) states that the Nihil Obstat and Imprimatur are no longer required on publications that deal with private revelations, provided they contain nothing contrary to faith and morals.

The publisher wishes to manifest unconditional submission to the final and official judgement of the Magisterium of the Church regarding the events presently under investigation at Oliveto Citra.

Cover Design: Art Mancuso

Published by:
    Franciscan University Press
    Franciscan University of Steubenville
    Steubenville, OH 43952

Printed in the United States of America

ISBN: 0-940535-20-3

FOR

Father René Laurentin

CONTENTS

NOTE TO THE READER

What we have written in this book is our own testimony, our own experience. The only authoritative judge of the validity and the authenticity of the apparitions, in general and in particular, at Oliveto Citra is the Church in the persons of the competent authorities, especially of the Archdiocese of Salerno, Italy, and of the Holy See in Rome.

Personally and subjectively, we are convinced of the general authenticity of these apparitions. We believe that Our Lady has come, is coming, in these days, to Oliveto Citra in Italy, and to the world. This is our personal judgment. Our purpose here, however, is not to judge but to report and reflect.

Robert Faricy, S.J.
Luciana Pecoraio
March 25, 1989

CHAPTER 1

THE BLESSED
VIRGIN MARY COMES
TO OLIVETO CITRA

Every evening the small square in front of the ruined medieval castle fills with pilgrims and with residents of Oliveto Citra, a small town in southern Italy. They recite the fifteen mysteries of the rosary. They sing hymns. They pray aloud.

And some of them, it seems, see the Blessed Virgin Mary; some, it seems, hear her speak.

Filomena comes every day at 4:15 on the bus from Salerno to see Our Lady. Umberto, a mechanic, sees her often at the castle gate. Eleven-year-old Marco sees her too.

So do others. Tourists. Pilgrims. People who live in Oliveto Citra. People from nearby towns. People from far away, from all over the world.

Over one hundred people have signed documents, now in the parish office, that they have seen Our Lady at the gate of the old castle. But many, perhaps hundreds of others, have seen her but have never written signed testimonies. Anna had never told anyone outside her family

7

that she sees Our Lady regularly. Pilgrims, present for one or two evenings, say they have seen her and then get on the tourist bus for home.

Do all these people really see the Blessed Virgin Mary? Do they really hear her speak? And if they do, what does she say to them, to the world, to us?

Can the apparitions at Oliveto Citra be authenticated, verified? What do they mean?

What is going on at Oliveto Citra?

Oliveto Citra

South of Naples, about one and one-half hours' drive going east from Salerno on the freeway and then moving north again on a regional road that winds through the hills, you can see Oliveto Citra (population about 3500) well before you get there. It sits on one end of a loaf-like hill, built for defense, the houses piled together in a heap and topped by the castle. Up close, you can see that much of the town was destroyed in the 1980 earthquake. Many families continue to live in temporary prefabricated dwellings.

The main industry here is farming. In most Italian communities the farmers live in towns, but here they live near the land. This explains the numerous white red-roofed houses dotting the valley of the Sele River below the town.

Oliveto Citra has one Catholic parish, one priest, Monsignor Giuseppe Amato, and, until recently, few practicing Catholics. In the municipal elections of May 1985, just before the apparitions began, the town voted nearly unanimously for a Communist mayor and a Communist town council.

The narrow streets of the town can hold only one car; they do not permit two-way traffic. The main street that runs through the town has a traffic light at each end to regulate automobiles so that traffic can flow in only one direction at a time.

The main street passes through the central square, Piazza Garibaldi, and then through a small unnamed square. To the right, just beyond the little square, you can see the baroque facade of the parish church, Our Lady of Mercy. The church, badly damaged during the earthquake of 1980, remained closed for several years for repairs. It reopened in December 1988.

Across from the old church, on higher ground, looms the castle. Built in 1145, used during World War II and after for drying animal skins, its ruins further destroyed by the 1980 earthquake, the castle stands locked up, closed to visitors. An old stone stairway leads from the little square up to a fence and gate made of vertical iron bars. A rusty chain and padlock hold the gate closed.

Inside the gate the branches of bushes hold rosaries of various colors. The bushes look like exotic plants with rosaries for fruit. Flowers line the walkway up from the gate along the wall of the castle.

This is where Our Lady comes every evening. And this is where the apparitions began in May 1985.

May 24, 1985

Saint Macarius, the patron saint of Oliveto Citra, has his feastday on May 24. About 10:00 p.m. on the feast of Saint Macarius, 1985, twelve small boys played in the little square just off Piazza Garibaldi. The townspeople had gathered in Piazza Garibaldi to celebrate the feast, which in Oliveto Citra takes the form of a civil rather than a religious observance. The music and singing filtered through the narrow passage between buildings where the main street connects the larger square to the small one where the boys played.

Suddenly the boys heard a baby crying. The baby's voice came from the other side of the old iron castle gate. Several of the boys, alarmed, frightened, excited, ran back and forth between the little square and Piazza Garibaldi. Finally one

9

boy threw a stone at the gate. The stone went inside the castle grounds, but seemed to strike nothing and not to fall to the ground. Frightened, the boys ran, then returned. And, almost immediately, a woman appeared. Or something. Different boys saw different things.

A few saw a light or a luminous shape, or a light shaped like a person. Several saw a young woman. Some saw an infant in her arms. Others did not. But they each saw something.

The twelve boys, all about ten to twelve years old, ran into the Iannece Bar in the Piazza Garibaldi shouting, "We've seen the Blessed Virgin Mary." Silvia Lullo, twenty-five years old, born and raised in Peterborough, England, behind the bar, believed them. Her assistant, Anita Rio, said, "Come on! How could these boys have seen the Blessed Virgin Mary?" The boys said, "It's true; come and see." And they ran back to the little square with the gate to the castle.

Anita Rio, curious, followed behind them. When she caught up with them at the castle gate, she saw, beyond the gate, a young woman of indescribable beauty dressed in a white robe and wearing a blue mantle with a filigreed gold border. A crown of stars encircled her head. She carried an infant in her right arm. The infant held a rosary in his hands.

Anita, frightened, backed up. The young woman motioned to her with her free hand, beckoned her to come forward. The woman said to Anita, "You will see me at night."

Anita was taken to the hospital in a state of shock. The doctor on duty, Giuseppe Santinelli, when told the apparent reason for her condition, asked her several questions to ascertain her general psychological state. His diagnosis: "This girl is healthy in body and in mind; she has an obvious muscular tension as though something has caused her

10

great fear.''

Early in 1986, we went to Oliveto Citra to learn about the events there. We spoke with some of the boys who had played in the small square and who had seen something on May 24. We spoke with Anita Rio and with many others, including the parish priest.

And in the evening we went to the castle gate in the little square to say the rosary, to sing hymns, to pray, to honor Our Lady. There we met Umberto and Filomena and others who see Our Lady frequently. We have returned many times to Oliveto Citra. We have come to know well several of the persons involved in the apparitions. And Luciana very often leads the weekly prayer meeting of those who see Our Lady, and gives the instruction, usually on personal prayer or on other elements of the spiritual life.

Here, in the chapters that follow, are our findings and our impressions concerning the events at Oliveto Citra. Obviously, we cannot make a final judgment as to the authenticity of those events. The Church will do that in due time and after the necessary formal investigations.

In the meantime, more and more people hear about Oliveto Citra, sometimes in a distorted way. More and more pilgrims go there. A brief, accurate description of what is happening at Oliveto Citra seems needed. Here are some of the results of our visits there: what we have seen, what people have told us, what we have experienced.

11

CHAPTER 2

OUR LADY OF THE CASTLE

Dino and Carmine

Two of the twelve boys who played in the small square the night of May 24, 1985, and who saw something are Dino and Carmine Acquaviva, fifteen-year-old twins who came to Oliveto from Chicago when their family moved to Italy in 1984. They speak both English and Italian.

We spoke with them in the kitchen of the apartment where they live with their two older brothers, and their parents, Gerardo and Rosaria Acquaviva. We spoke in both Italian and English. They are good, healthy, normal boys. They have had a Catholic upbringing, with religious education and regular church attendance. Their mother said that they have always had religious faith but that they have never been fanatical in any way.

We asked them to describe what happened the night of May 24, 1985. Carmine spoke:

> The twenty-fourth of May we were in the piazza [Garibaldi] for the feast of Saint Macarius, the patron of this town. We were behind the stage where there was a magician who scared us, and we ran away.

13

We ran up to the little square. We heard crying there, and we all ran away. Then we returned out of curiosity. An eleven-year-old boy, Angelo Grieco, threw a stone. It didn't hit anything. Then there came a louder crying and we ran away again.

Then Dino and Gerardo Cavalieri went toward the crying. We were quiet. Then we saw a little light that became bigger and bigger, and exploded. There was so much light. Then Our Lady came. She seemed at first like a form or a shape. She came forward a little at a time. She was dressed in white with a sky-blue mantle that had a golden stripe on the front, and a crown of stars.''

Luciana asked Carmine what Our Lady's face was like.

Carmine: I couldn't see it. Her arm held a baby; the baby was crying.

Luciana: Did she say anything?

Carmine: She said, 'Peace to you, children.'

Like Carmine, Dino too saw Our Lady with the Infant Jesus. in her arms. But, unlike Carmine, Dino also saw the devil, or the head of the devil, just under Our Lady's feet. This frightened him.

Carmine: What reaction did you have?

Luciana: Fear; we ran away.

Dino and Carmine Acquaviva speak freely and openly of their experiences. They continued to see Our Lady at the castle gate frequently, several evenings a week, for more than a month after the first time. And they have seen her occasionally after that.

In particular, on August 24, 1985, a little after ten in the evening, Our Lady appeared to them at the gate of the castle.

Dino asked her, "In the name of the Most Holy Trinity, who are you?" She replied, "I am Our Lady of Graces."

The next evening, August 25, Dino and Carmine saw her again at the castle gate. "It was about nine o'clock," Carmine told me, "that I went up the castle. There were already some people from out of town there to see if they could see something. I went off a little by myself and said some 'Hail Mary's.' After praying I lifted my head and saw Our Lady. She was at the other end of the walkway, dressed in a white robe, not too shiny. I asked her in the name of the Most Holy Trinity which Madonna are you? And she answered, 'I am Our Lady of Consolation.'

"I asked Our Lady, 'What should we do?' The answer was, 'Pray, pray, pray.' "

Rosaria Acquaviva worries about her two sons. "They're at a sensitive age," she says. But both Dino and Carmine seem normal, even ordinary, and quite healthy.

Anita

Anita Rio is twenty-four years old, pretty, forthright, and practical. She is the second of six children. When we first met her in 1985, she lived with her mother, Angelina, and the other children in a small house, without plumbing and without electricity, several miles from Oliveto Citra in the large valley. Anita's father died at Christmas time, 1985.

Anita married Lorenzo Gasparro on April 20, 1986. She no longer works at the Iannece bar. She lives outside Oliveto Citra with her husband and two-year-old girl, Sara.

When we first spoke with Anita, she saw Our Lady regularly two or three times a week, always at the castle gate, except on May 25, 1985, the night after the first apparition, when she appeared to Anita at home. On that night Anita asked Our Lady, "Why have you chosen me?" Mary answered, "I have not chosen only you, because many will see me, but there will remain only those who have the

15

courage to believe.''

Luciana talked with Anita. Here is a transcription, translated from the Italian, of what she said:

Anita: That evening I was working in the bar. We'd seen Dino and Carmine who said they'd seen Our Lady, and I laughed because I didn't believe them. The people in the bar said, "Anita, do you know they saw Our Lady?" "Come on," I said; I even laughed. I went there and I was thinking that they all see her, because this American boy who was fainting, was holding on to his father's hand, and they were all crying.

Luciana: Dino was the one that was fainting?

Anita: Yes. I was thinking maybe they've all seen her, but she hasn't said anything to me. I went back to the bar. Then I went back and looked again. Then another time. And then I don't remember because that night they took me to the hospital; I don't remember that night anymore.

Luciana: They took you to the hospital?

Anita: Yes.

Luciana: You were sick?

Anita: Yes.

Luciana: How did you feel?

Anita: I don't remember anything about how I felt.

Luciana: The others say you saw what they saw.

Anita: That's enough. I don't remember. After that I saw her many times, not every time I went there.

Luciana: What did you see exactly, and how did she look the first time?

Anita: A figure dressed in white with a sky-blue mantle holding a child in her arm with a rosary

Luciana: She held a rosary, or the baby?

16

Anita: The baby had a rosary in his hand.

Luciana: Was she standing still?

Anita: She was moving, coming toward us.

Luciana: Was she smiling?

Anita: She had a young face.

Luciana: Did she say anything?

Anita: To pray. She wanted a chapel.

Luciana: She said she wanted a chapel?

Anita: Yes.

Luciana: She told you she wanted a chapel and nothing else?

Anita: Yes. Also, to pray.

Luciana: How did she tell you to pray?

Anita: ''Pray, pray, pray.''

Luciana: How many times did she tell you?

Anita: Three times.

Luciana: When you asked her who she was she told you what you should call her?

Anita: Our Lady of the Castle. ''I am our Lady of the Castle.'' Because they told me to say, ''Who are you, in the name of the Most Holy Trinity?''

Luciana: Who told you to say that? Priests, or the people who were there?

Anita: The people there.

Luciana: And she answered?

Anita: ''I am Our Lady of the Castle.''

Luciana: For you personally, did she give you any suggestion, did she say anything?

Anita: Yes, but I can't say.

Luciana: She gave you some secret message?

Anita: Yes.

Our Lady told Anita that she wanted a small chapel at the castle gate on at least two other occasions. On May 28, the third time Anita saw Our Lady, she smelled a beautiful perfume that she had never smelled before. From then on, she always smells it when she sees Our Lady. And Mary said to Anita, ''I want a chapel for everyone in this place where you see me.'' And on June 22, feeling drawn to go to the castle gate, Anita saw Our Lady and asked her, ''Tell me what I can do for you.'' Mary answered, ''I want the chapel; I have told this to others too.''

On August 5, 1985, Our Lady appeared to Anita dressed in shining gold and carrying roses. When Anita asked her why she was dressed like that, she said, ''Today is a day to celebrate; it's my birthday.''

Anita has received secret messages, which Our Lady told her to share with no one. Many times Our Lady has appeared to Anita without saying anything.

Mary does not appear to Anita now as often as in 1985. In 1987, Anita saw Our Lady about every two months, always at the castle gate and she continued to receive messages from her, some personal and some about the future of the world. Since January 1, 1988, Anita has not seen Our Lady.

The chapel that Mary asked for now stands next to the gate of the castle. A tiny structure, it has just the space for a statue of Our Lady that faces out through a large glass window shaped like a star. Don Peppino blessed and dedicated the little chapel in April 1987, with the knowledge of Archbishop Grimaldi of Salerno, who considers it a private initiative not needing any official church authorization or permission.

The beautiful statue of Mary, in marble of different colors, by the Italian sculptor Ludovico Bertoni, shows Our Lady holding the Infant Jesus. Just as so many who have seen her at Oliveto have described her, she wears a white dress and a blue mantle with gold filigree. The infant in her arms has a rosary in his hand.

CHAPTER 3

AT THE CASTLE GATE

A cold wind blows through the little square on this particular January evening when we come to pray at the gate of the castle. We have come fairly late. Already, about 5:30 this evening, a large group has met to say all fifteen mysteries of the rosary, to sing hymns, and to pray in the square and at the top of the steps at the castle gate.

Tonight is quiet. Last night, Sunday, more than twenty bus-loads of pilgrims came. And the "Evangelicals" came, members of an American-financed pentecostal church here in Oliveto Citra. They come from time to time to heckle. Many of them are members of the Christian Democratic Party, and all of them are believing Christians. They love Jesus but they hate what's going on at the castle gate. When they come, they stand apart, shout abuses, and try to drown out the Catholic singing with their own hymns. But tonight they stayed home.

Praying at the Castle Gate

At 8:30 the rosary begins. We go right through all fifteen mysteries, led by people speaking through a microphone hooked up to amplifiers in the square. We pray in a group of about one hundred eighty people. Our backs to the buildings behind us, we face the gate to the castle and the stone stair leading up to it. The ruins of the ancient Norman castle stand over us on the right. Piazza Garibaldi is on our left. An occasional automobile following the main street through town passes between us and the stairway to the castle gate.

After the rosary, we say the litany of Our Lady. It all takes about an hour and ten minutes.

People go to the gate to pray for a few minutes after the rosary and the litany. But only eight or ten people at a time can go to the gate because the gate is only ten feet wide. I go in the first shift of ten people. I do pray at the gate. But I also look around to see what the others are doing. I notice one man in particular, in work clothes, who seems immobilized as though in an ecstasy. I will meet him later back down in the square.

A young man regulates the traffic. After my shift has prayed at the gate for four or five minutes, he calls us to return into the square, and he moves the next shift of ten people up to the gate.

In the meantime, while a few people pray at the castle gate, the others sing hymns, pray, and have a kind of prayer meeting. Monsignor Giuseppe Amato, the parish pastor, known locally and with great affection as Don Peppino, gives a short talk. He says that pilgrims should not be disappointed if they do not see Our Lady; she is here with us, present to us.

Queen of the Castle

We know most of the hymns that the group sings. But one hymn, quite long, we have never heard before. It is called, "Queen of the Castle," and it is a hymn to Our Lady. Here is the story behind the hymn.

In the fall of 1985, Albino Coglianese who was head of the

parish committee that leads the evening prayer and collects written testimonies, wrote the words to "Queen of the Castle" so that they could be sung to an old southern Italian folk melody. The hymn has seven fairly long verses.

One Tuesday evening, October 29, 1985, at 8:45, Mafalda Caputo took the microphone in the little piazza in order to lead the rosary. Before she could begin, she saw a luminous shape and heard Our Lady's voice inviting her to sing the hymn, "Queen of the Castle." Mafalda found the words to the hymn and began to lead the singing. She started the first verse singing the folk melody, according to the way that the hymn had been sung up to that moment.

She heard Our Lady say, "Don't sing it that way; listen to the choir and learn the melody and teach it to the others." Mafalda did not see any choir, but she heard the hymn sung by beautiful voices, at first distant and then coming closer. She listened and learned the melody and taught it to those present.

Not only Mafalda heard the heavenly choir. In the parish office are documents signed by several persons of various ages stating that they too heard the invisible choir sing Albino Coglianese's hymn, "Queen of the Castle," to a new melody. Several weeks later, Our Lady told Mafalda that the melody sung by the choir in heaven is an ancient and long-forgotten melody of the region around Oliveto Citra.

"Queen of the Castle" has become the song of those who come to the castle gate in the little square. They sing it now, of course, with the melody taught by the heavenly choir, every night.

The praying and hymn-singing ends about 10:00. Some people leave, but most stay in the little square to talk or to pray by themselves. Some go up to the castle gate to pray.

Filomena

We meet Filomena Palmieri, whom Luciana already

knows, a woman about forty years old, who comes to the little square every evening. She makes the two-hour ride on the two-fifteen bus from Salerno. Filomena is married and has two sons studying medicine and commercial economy at the university. She sees Our Lady every evening.

This evening, at about 5:00, Our Lady told Filomena to speak to a group of pilgrims from Fatto Maggiore, a town near Naples. ''Tell them I bless every one of them, and that I will put peace and prayer in their homes.'' Filomena spoke to the pilgrims, and learned that a boy in the group had seen Our Lady just a few minutes before.

Donato

And I meet the man who was with me praying right at the castle gate after the rosary and litany. Donato Bracigliano is a worker with the Borselli Construction Company, building a new highway a few miles from Oliveto Citra. In the little square with Donato are two of his daughters, Anna, thirteen, and Rafaelina, twelve. The next day we meet his wife and six beautiful children at their pleasant home outside the town.

Here is Luciana's conversation with Donato:

Luciana: They tell me that you see Our Lady.

Donato: Yes.

Luciana: Every evening?

Donato: Yes.

Luciana: When you see her, what does she say? How does she appear? The first time, for instance.

Donato: The first time I saw her was November 2. There was a lot of light. Our Lady came up close to me, and she said to me, ''Donato, go and get the sick man in the wheelchair.'' I took him in my arms and I brought him close to the gate. Our Lady told me she wanted to touch him with her hands. He saw her too.

24

She had a white dress and a blue mantle, and a child in her arms, and a rosary. We stayed until three. Another time I went with another sick man and Our Lady was there and the sick man saw her and asked her to heal him. It was a Sunday about nine-thirty; she told me to go and get him and carry him close to the gate. I was in touch with him up until December 8. Now he walks and he's healed.

Luciana: What did the doctors say? Were they surprised?

Donato: Yes.

Luciana: Was there referral to a doctor?

Donato: Yes.

Luciana: Was the illness incurable?

Donato: Yes, he couldn't move, and he was completely disabled since birth.

Luciana: Did you have faith before you saw Our Lady?

Donato: Well, . . .

Luciana: Has anything changed in your life?

Donato: Yes, I feel stronger, more protected.

Donato saw Our Lady every day from November 2, 1985 until August 12, 1987. Since then, she has not appeared to him. When we asked him why he thinks he hasn't seen her, he said perhaps because he doesn't pray enough.

Late Night in the Little Square

At 10:30, as it does every evening at this time, the parish committee for the apparitions meets to evaluate how the evening went. One by one, they go up the stairway of Number Twelve in the little square, directly opposite the castle gate, to the committee office.

The committee has ten members: eight men of the parish; the priest, Don Peppino; and Anna De Bellis, the mother of two small children who see Our Lady frequently. Albino Coglianesi, who wrote the words for the hymn, "Queen of the Castle," coordinated the committee at the time of our visit.

Albino is a heavyset, middle-aged man with a full grey beard. He moves slowly and speaks deliberately. He works as a surveyor and building consultant, and was chairman of the local Socialist Party for seven years. Recently, he formed a small group of "Christians for Socialism."

There are a number of things to discuss this evening. Four pilgrims have turned in written witnesses saying that they saw Our Lady tonight at the castle gate; these need to be evaluated and turned over to the parish priest, Don Peppino. And there are several items held over from previous meetings.

A man enters the office to make a financial contribution. A committee member tells him that his money will go toward the building of a small chapel near the castle gate, and gives him a receipt. Every contribution here is recorded, and every donor is given a receipt.

Before the committee meeting begins, we leave to go back down into the little square. Several people still stand around. Some pray at the gate. We turn left down the short connecting street to Piazza Garibaldi and go into the Iannece bar. Michael Lullo, the proprietor, won't let us pay for our coffee.

We walk back to the castle gate. It is now almost midnight. Several people still pray there.

CHAPTER 4

THEY SEE THE MOTHER OF JESUS

In the parish at Oliveto Citra, Don Peppino says there are about twenty persons to whom Our Lady has appeared several times. There is as yet no fixed group of "visionaries"; it has not settled yet. Perhaps some who have seen Our Lady several times may stop seeing her, or have already stopped. Others may go on seeing her for some time. Maybe, eventually, there will be a fixed group of people at Oliveto Citra whom Our Lady visits with a certain frequency.

There is, however, no group like the children at Fatima or like the small group at Medjugorje in Yugoslavia. There seems to be no particular unity among the people Our Lady has chosen at Oliveto Citra. The only common points of reference are Our Lady herself and Don Peppino.

Besides Carmine and Dino Acquaviva, Anita Rio, Donato Bracigliano, and Filomena Palmieri, we met and talked with a number of other persons who see Our Lady regularly. In particular, we met a young brother and sister, an automobile mechanic, a sixteen-year-old girl from a nearby town, a housewife and mother, and a nineteen-year-old young man who works as a carpenter.

Sabrina and Marco

Sabrina De Bellis is thirteen years old. Her brother, Marco, is eleven. They both have seen Our Lady many times. Sabrina and Marco live with their parents, Agostino and Anna De Bellis, and their little brother, Andrea, five, in a spacious apartment in Oliveto Citra. Dr. De Bellis is a dentist.

Sabrina and Marco say the rosary every day, all fifteen mysteries. Sometimes they pray together in the room of one of them. Sometimes, especially in the car when their father is driving, they pray the rosary with their mother, Anna.

Anna has never seen Our Lady, but almost every day she sees, from the window of the apartment, a light at or near the castle. She thinks it's Our Lady. Also, she frequently smells a perfume in the apartment, something like the smell of roses; twice she has smelled incense. She receives interior locations from Our Lady, messages that invite her and everyone to continuous conversion, to prayer, and to penance.

Sabrina and Marco have also smelled the perfume. This phenomenon is common at Oliveto Citra. Many people, including Luciana, have smelled the perfume in the area around the castle gate.

Dr. De Bellis saw Our Lady once, on July 20, 1985. On that evening more than two thousand people were in the little square. The word had been passed that something special would happen that evening at eleven o'clock. At eleven, a cloud, colored bright red and illuminated by the searchlights that light up the castle ruins, descended on the castle and circled it and the buildings near it. Everyone saw it, including people in other parts of the town and outside the town. And many people heard a woman's voice coming from the gate. It said, "I have sent this cloud as the first sign." And about fifty people, including Dr. De Bellis, saw Our Lady.

28

Sabrina first saw Our Lady in June 1985, one evening at the gate of the castle. The vision lasted several hours and Sabrina clung to the gate and would not leave despite the lateness of the hour. Finally, a man in the crowd around Sabrina, Dr. Luigi Mirto, gave her three questions to ask Our Lady. He dictated them to Sabrina in German, a language she cannot understand at all. Sabrina repeated the questions to Our Lady and relayed the answers, which came to her in Italian.

Question (in German): Are you the mother of everyone?

Answer (in Italian): Yes.

Question (in German): What message do you want us to take to everyone?

Answer (in Italian): Pray, pray, pray.

Question (in German): How old are you? (To this silly question no answer came.)

Besides saying the full rosary every day, Sabrina spends time daily praying for various intentions, especially for sick people. She also prays for sinners, for the world, for peace, and for other intentions. Sabrina sees Our Lady often, although she sometimes goes for long periods of time, even for several months, without seeing her . On Wednesday, November 13, 1985, at 6:30 p.m. at the castle gate, Sabrina saw the Blessed Virgin and received a five-point message from her. Sabrina has given us permission to quote the following:

I went up to the castle and I saw Our Lady dressed in white, near the gate, and she dictated to me five messages. They are: (1) All the pilgrims who come to me I will bless and I will purify; (2) The world should pray because prayer is declining; (3) To those who come together in prayer I will send my Son, the Savior. (4) This place is sacred, and I want a little chapel outside the gate with an image of me in it. (5) I thank all who have decorated this place with flowers, and whoever arranges them will be purified of their sins.

Sabrina also told us we could quote some messages. On February 2, 1986, the Blessed Virgin Mary gave Sabrina this message:

People who pray will not fall into the abyss that hell holds, but they will go up to the kingdom of heaven, they will see the magnificent fields of brotherly love, and they will be able to see the heavenly paradise. They will greatly marvel at its beauty. They will be happy. They will visit all of paradise, including the great hall of judgment where each of them will be judged. They will exult and go wild with joy, and they will reign next to me and to God for eternity.

The next day Our Lady told Sabrina, "All of you should pray, pray, pray, and trust in me, dear children; I will help you in all dangers, and I will console you in every moment of anguish." And on February 10, this message: "My children, come close to my faith, be converted, and do not worry about your problems; I will help you and I will watch over you from the kingdom of heaven."

On November 6, 1987, Our Lady appeared to Sabrina at the castle gate. She was dressed in white, her hands were open, and her feet rested on a white cloud. Sabrina saw a bright light come from Our Lady and descend on everyone there at the gate. Our Lady raised her hands and said:

My children, come to me; open your hearts and they will be filled with good things. Jesus is with you, together with me, to save you from temptation. Satan becomes always stronger; pray that he loses his power and that you all grow closer to God. The evil one has taken over many; but do not be afraid, my Son will free them...Pray not to enter into temptation. Now I bless you all in the name of the Father, the Son, and the Holy Spirit.

After that, Sabrina saw her blow a kiss and disappear in a very bright light.

Sabrina and Marco were praying together on December 20, 1988 when they both saw a strong light. In the light, Marco saw a rose-colored cloud with writing on it: "If you continue to follow the path you are on, the gates of paradise will be open." And he heard Mary tell him to read the sentence carefully until it disappeared. Sabrina, at the same time, saw Our Lady, dressed in a white robe and a blue mantle, with the Infant Jesus in her arms. Our Lady said to Sabrina, "Have faith even when you do not see me; I will stay close to you and give you signs that I am present next to you."

Sabrina is a bright girl, mature for her age, poised and direct in her manner. Marco is more shy, but quite active. He has bright red hair and does not long stay in one place. He says he wants to be a priest.

Marco sees Our Lady almost every day. Often, she comes to him at night, waking him up. The first time Marco saw her, in 1985, he saw a woman on the balcony of the apartment where his family lives. She stood on a small cloud, very tall, brown eyes, and with a child in her arms, and a very long rosary in her hand. She smiled at him. He knew that he was looking at Our Lady.

Marco sometimes sees angels. And sometimes he sees the devil who occasionally tries to pull him out of bed. He disappears when Marco hits him with his rosary. Mary has shown Marco both heaven and hell in visions. And she has given Marco nine secrets; he refuses to talk about them.

Here are some recent messages Our Lady has given to Marco. On April 15, 1988, she told him, "I will use you and the others who see me as witnesses for unbelievers; be simple, humble, and obedient. Now I bless you in the name of the Father, the Son, and the Holy Spirit." Later the same day, she appeared to Marco again and gave him this message, "My children, the world stands already at the edge of the abyss; try to pray and to be detached from the things of this world, otherwise you will not find acceptance into the kingdom of heaven." A few days later, Our Lady said to Marco, "I am the Immaculate Virgin Mother of God."

On September 17, 1988, during the weekly prayer meeting of those who see Our Lady at Oliveto Citra, Our Lady told Marco, "For a while you won't see me anymore; your suffering will help many people." Then, during the meeting two weeks later, she spoke to him again, "Marco, soon you'll see me again." He began to see her again twelve days after that. At the time of this writing, he sees her every time he prays. On January 9, 1989, she thanked everyone, through Marco, for their prayers and for the meditated rosary.

Andrea, Sabrina's and Marco's five-year-old brother, has seen Our Lady several times, and, often, Jesus crucified. His visions began when he was three. He talks about them almost not at all except to his family.

Umberto

On the east edge of Oliveto Citra, just before you go up the incline to the top of the hill where the castle rises above the town, on the right side of the road is Umberto Gagliardi's Alfa-Romeo garage. Umberto works here with two assistants. He lives in an apartment, in the same building as the garage, with his wife and three teen-aged children.

When I came to talk to him at his garage, Umberto, wearing blue coveralls, was giving instructions to two young mechanics in identical coveralls. He is a pleasant-looking man about forty years old.

Until June 1985, Umberto did not practice his Catholic faith. He went to Mass about once a year. He seems to have had no religious instruction, and even now he does not read religious books of any kind. Umberto heard about the apparitions at the castle gate when they began at the end of May 1985. They held no interest for him at all.

On June 2, Umberto went to the little square to go to the pharmacy there. Before he arrived at the pharmacy door, he suddenly saw coming toward him a luminous cloud in the shape of a woman. The sight gave him a great shock and left him with a bad headache. He felt terrible and sought help in the pharmacy. In succeeding days, he went to the little square in the evening, and Our Lady appeared to him as a kind of luminous form of a person, but clearer than the first time. But, in these apparitions too, Umberto felt shock, and he trembled and broke out in perspiration. Finally, after a while, Our Lady began to appear to him as a normal person, but very beautiful and with a radiant luminosity.

Umberto sees Our Lady almost always at the gate of the castle. And he sees her every time he goes to the castle gate. He goes often, but not every evening. Only three times has he seen her in other places: once in a nearby wood; once the Sunday after Christmas 1985, at Mass, "all in white, praying for us with her hands joined"; and once, in early January 1986 when driving in a car with three other men, near his Alfa-Romeo garage. He saw Our Lady over the castle; he told the others; they stopped the car, and Umberto had the vision for about an hour.

But ordinarily he sees her in the little square. He says that she dresses "like a nun," wearing a white dress and a blue veil. After the first few times he saw her, she always spoke to him when she appeared to him. The messages have been sometimes secrets, sometimes for individual people, and sometimes predictions of things to come. Umberto says they always come true. Often the message is for Umberto, and to everyone through him, to pray, pray, pray, to help Our Lady to pray for conversions, to pray for the world.

When he drives, Umberto always sees a strong light in front of the car. He thinks it's Our Lady going ahead of him and guiding him.

Umberto has seen Jesus four times, once seated at a table with twelve men, and once wearing a crown of thorns. All four times Jesus was dressed in white, had long hair, wore sandals, and looked at Umberto in silence.

On some occasions Our Lady has given Umberto her hand and has shaken hands with him. He says that her hand is normal, with the same warmth as anyone else's hand.

Not everyone believes that Umberto sees Our Lady. This causes him pain, but he lives with it.

Umberto says he has changed a lot since he began to see Our Lady. He goes to Mass every Sunday. He prays every day, and says the rosary at home with his family, and often at the castle gate in the evening. He checks regularly with his spiritual director, Don Peppino.

He says he has a different outlook on life now, and lives it differently from before. He tries not to do any wrong, and if someone wrongs him or refuses to greet him, he greets the other person anyway. And he adds that his family is happy with the ways things are going.

Antonella

Coming from Salerno, going south and inland, four or five miles before you get to Oliveto Citra, you come to the town of Contursi Terme. Antonella Giordano, sixteen years old, lives here. A pretty girl, poised and friendly, obviously intelligent, she sees Our Lady regularly.

We went to the parish church of Contursi Terme where we met the pastor, Father Salvatore Siani, a member of the archdiocesan commission that has investigated the events at Oliveto Citra. He directed us to Antonella's home. We spent a couple of hours with her. She has a spiritual maturity remarkable in a person her age, or any age.

Antonella heard about the apparition of Our Lady at the gate of the castle the day after the first apparition, but she did not believe in it. However, she went there with her mother a few days later and prayed with the group in the little square. Then, on Saturday, June 1, she saw Our Lady at the gate of the castle. Here is what she told Luciana in 1985:

Antonella: While I was praying there together with Gerardo Cavalieri, he said that he saw Our Lady, and I saw her too, dressed in black.

Luciana: In black?

Antonella: Yes, she was Our Lady of Sorrows and she had her hands joined and she was kneeling. Then I went other evenings, and I saw her almost always.

Luciana: What did you see? Our lady only, or other things too?

Antonella: I saw ugly things too.

Luciana: What does Our Lady look like?

Antonella: When I see her now, she's almost always dressed in white. The first times in black, and then she said she was Our Lady of Sorrows. We have that statue in the cemetery here at Contursi.

Luciana: Did you have much faith before?

Antonella: Yes, but I didn't believe it when Our Lady first came.

Luciana: And after your visions?

Antonella: I'm different than I was before.

Luciana: How do you feel inside?

Antonella: Happier and happier.

Luciana: Has Our Lady said anything to you?

Antonella: Yes, she told me to pray. She said, ''You should pray so that nothing happens to you.'' She hasn't given me any message. The first times I saw her she said that we should fast on Fridays on bread and water.

Luciana: Why?

Antonella: She didn't say.

Luciana: When you talked about ugly things, what did you mean?

Antonella: The devil.

Luciana: Did you recognize him?

Antonella: Yes. I'd seen pictures of him at school; but Our Lady had warned me.

Luciana: Were you frightened?

Antonella: A lot.

Luciana: What did he say to you?

Antonella: He didn't say anything, only one time he said he'd make something happen to me.

Luciana: What did you do?

Antonella: I ran away.

Luciana: How did you free yourself from seeing the devil?

Antonella: With the rosary.

Luciana: And what did you say?

Antonella: ''In the name of the Most Holy Trinity.''

Luciana: Somebody taught you that?

Antonella: No.

Luciana: Are you sure that seeing Our Lady is not the work of your imagination?

Antonella: Yes.

Luciana: What would you say to someone to convince them of the truth?

Antonella: I don't know.

Luciana: Do you see Our Lady at home?

Antonella: I've seen her here only four times, but she didn't say anything, she smiled.

Luciana: Is it going well at school?

Antonella: Yes.

Luciana: How have your schoolmates taken this?

Antonella: I don't know; there are some that believe and some that don't believe.

Luciana: Some that make fun of you?

Antonella: Yes.

Luciana: Have any of your schoolmates come to see?

Antonella: No, nobody.

Luciana: You're really happy about this thing?

Antonella: Yes.

Antonella sees Mary especially when she goes to the castle gate, about twice a month. Perhaps because Antonella finds it difficult to get from her house in nearby Contursi Terme to Oliveto Citra, and cannot go often, Our Lady appears to her sometimes in her home where she lives with her family. Antonella has quit school and works as a waitress in a Contursi Terme restaurant.

She prays regularly, contemplatively, in the morning and again in the evening, says the rosary daily, and fasts on Fridays. She finds it easy to pray during the day while she works at home or at the restaurant.

Antonella continues to receive messages from Our Lady. She has received three secrets, one for the world and two regarding her own life. She says Our Lady will show her when and how she should reveal them. And Our Lady frequently gives her messages, tells her things.

We have Antonella's permission to quote from her diary.

Here are two excerpts from the summer and fall of 1986 that are typical:

I went to Oliveto July 19, 1986, with Luciana Pecoraio. We went to Mass at 7 p.m.; at 9 p.m. we began the rosary at the castle gate. Mrs. De Bellis called me because I was supposed to lead the rosary. I said in my mind, ''Mary, help me because I'm nervous in front of so many people.'' I went; Mrs. De Bellis, Mafalda, and another lady were there. When I began the rosary, Our Lady suggested in my ear how I should pray, but I didn't see her. After having finished the rosary, I passed the microphone to another woman because I did not feel well. Then suddenly I went into ecstasy. I asked Our Lady, ''Why haven't I seen you for such a long time?'' She answered, ''Don't be worried.'' Then I asked her, ''Do you accept the prayers that I make to you every evening and will I receive that grace I ask for always?'' She answered, ''Yes, I accept your prayers, but for that grace you'll have to wait,'' and then she said goodbye, after which I came to. I had a headache. I went to where Luciana was and we left together.

I went to Oliveto September 8, 1986; at the gate there were two bus-loads of nuns. When we got there they had already begun the rosary. I went up the steps with Little Andrew (De Bellis); after a while he fell asleep and I carried him to his mother. I went back up with Marilena (Antonella's little sister) and Filomena. While I was praying, I heard Our Lady's voice. She said to me, ''Antonella, I want you to come here more often.'' I didn't see anything. Then I fell, and after two or three minutes I came to and saw the sisters. I began to cry, and heard Our Lady say to me, ''Your prayers are very valuable; pray for drug addicts, prisoners, unmarried mothers, and for people who are criticized by others;

goodbye, I love you''; and then I didn't hear her anymore. After a while my mother called me to go...

CHAPTER 5

MESSAGES FROM OUR LADY

As the last chapter shows, some who frequently see Our Lady also receive messages. Two of the people who receive important messages are Tarcisio Di Biasi and Mafalda Caputo.

Tarcisio

Tarcisio Di Biasi, nineteen years old, lives at Oliveto Citra with his mother, his grandmother, and his brother. A tall, good-looking young man, he worked as a carpenter before he went into the army. Tarcisio speaks matter-of-factly about seeing Our Lady. He has seen her several times. Many times he has written down what he saw and heard, signed it, and given the statement to Monsignor Amato. With Tarcisio's permission, I quote here extensively from those documents. Tarcisio writes:

> On the evening of May 24th I saw Our Lady. She was dressed with a white dress and a sky-blue veil and she had a child in her arm and the child had a rosary in his left hand. The first words that she said to me were, "Pray." Then she said that she had come to Oliveto Citra because there was so little faith. Then she

said that when Albino Coglianese prayed she heard him...

The evening of the 26th I saw Our Lady again. She asked me where was Anita, but Anita couldn't come.

The above is the first document, written by hand on two small sheets torn from a notebook, that Tarcisio gave to Monsignor Amato. Here is the second:

My name is Tarcisio Di Biasi, I am sixteen years old, and here is the story of my visions of Our Lady...insofar as I can remember, because I don't remember some things anymore.

On May 24th, the feastday of Saint Macarius, the patron of Oliveto Citra, I didn't go the piazza because I was very tired after the day's work. The following day, the 25th, when I went down to the piazza, they told me that the day before some boys had seen Our Lady over behind the gate of the old castle; right then I was very skeptical, and then I began to laugh and to joke.

In the evening, still in that state of skepticism, I went with some other boys up the steps that lead to the old castle; one boy, who was next to me, said, "I believe in it." I said, "You believe in these things at your age?" I hadn't even finished saying these words when I saw her, Our Lady, almost the whole person except that I couldn't make out her face which was like clouded over.

I began to cry, and I ran down the steps very emotional, and I found the mother of the twins, Carmine and Dino, who asked me why was I crying. I explained it all to her. She listened to me and gently brought me back up the steps, and I saw Our Lady again, and everything she said to me I can't remember, but I told the pastor, Don Peppino, everything and he taped it.

Right up until today, the devil has often threatened

me and tried to make me believe that a lot of bad things happen in the world through my fault. Several times when I wanted to go to the castle he made me feel so bad that sometimes I didn't think I was going to make it. But I found a strong weapon against him: prayer. This is the strongest thing that could exist; he has to run away, necessarily, because only God is trustful.

My life is changed, from that day I feel different. I don't want to be anymore with some boys who were bad company. I think a lot about how to help other people, about what they find hard; the sufferings of my neighbor have become my own sufferings. I want to add that, before I saw Our Lady, I blasphemed and I didn't go to church. Now all that is changed. One time I saw Our Lady weeping for me.

Oliveto Citra
November 23, 1985

In a later and undated document, Tarcisio writes that Our Lady sometimes appears to him at night before he goes to sleep.

She looks at me and I look at her. Often she smiles. And I tell her things about myself, and she gives me advice about what to do. She tells me not to be discouraged if something goes wrong because she is with me. She also tells me to help my neighbor; because I have had the good fortune to see her, I should help others to believe. And I shouldn't let it bother me that some don't believe, but I should continue on my way.

One time Our Lady asked me what do I choose to do with my life, to be a priest, or to get married. I answered her that I preferred to get married, and she said that was fine. Often she answers me when I recommend to her different people who ask me to and through her I can give comfort to these people with the words that she gives me to say.

One time I asked her what would she like from the people of Oliveto, and she answered me that they should pray, pray, pray. She also gave me some secret messages; there are four of them: one is for a person in Oliveto, the other three I cannot tell anyone; they are in fact warnings for mankind about which I am informed.

We should pray because with prayer we can ward off any calamity. I'm shaken and I can't sleep at night when I receive these messages and I suffer a lot for all mankind. Our Lady told me that she is very sad because in the world people do not pray enough.

On two sheets of paper dated December 15, 1985, Tarcisio has written the following:

I, the undersigned, Tarcisio Di Biasi of Oliveto Citra, declare that about nine p.m., while I was helping out keeping order near the gate, Our Lady appeared to me . . . and she said to me, ''Tell the pilgrims that I do not need flowers and candles, that I need prayers because the time left before the catastrophe is very short.''

A sheet of paper, handwritten and dated December 20, 1985, reads:

I, the undersigned, Tarcisio Di Biasi, at 8:45 p.m. had an apparition of Our Lady. She told me that the arm of her Son is held back, but we should remember that what the Lord has put in the world he can remove.

Here are the contents of two documents from January 1986. The first is dated January 12, 1986:

I, the undersigned, Tarcisio De Biasi, born at Oliveto Citra on June 12, 1969, and now living on Felice Caval-lotti Street, prefabricated area number two, declare that on January 12, 1986, at about ten minutes after ten at night, I saw Our Lady who said to me: ''Tell the

44

pilgrims not to be afraid of the messages; they have nothing to fear because they believe in my Son." Then she greeted me, saying, "I greet you in the name of the Father, the Son, and the Holy Spirit."

In the moment in which she disappeared, the devil appeared to me; he had a terrifying appearance. He had a head and a body like a goat's; he had a hunch-back. He said, "I finally caught you by surprise." And he threw at me a spear that he had in his hands.

Our Lady was dressed as usual. That is, she had a white tunic with a sky-blue mantle, but she did not hold a child.

The other document is dated January 17, 1986. It reads as follows:

I, the undersigned, Di Biasi, Tarcisio, at 9:20 p.m. in front of the gate, had an apparition of Our Lady and she told me that what was happening was our fault (many catastrophes are coming). To avoid all this we must pray. But all this, we have asked for it, because the Lord has given us many, many things, among them the earth, the oceans, the animals, intelligence, and many other things. And we have thought only about destroying them. If you do not pray, it will be inevitable...

On February 1, 1986, Tarcisio saw Our Lady a short distance from the gate, and, referring to the recitation of the rosary in common, she gave him this message: "My children, how happy I am when you pray together." Then she raised her arms to heaven and prayed, "My Son, see these persons who pray, have mercy on them." While she was looking upward she was wrapped in a dazzling light.

The night of May 1, 1986, Tarcisio wrote an account for the parish files of a vision he had had:

I went to the gate about 7:30 p.m. and stood to one side to pray. All of a sudden I felt like in an ecstasy or like I was fainting. Our Lady came and took me by the hand; she led me to an enormous door where there was a person with a beard and white hair. He opened the door and I went in with Our Lady. I saw a huge field with an infinity of flowers. There were a lot of people dressed in white, among whom I recognized Pinuzzo Roia who smiled and greeted me. Then we walked through the field and at the end, in a little blue cloud I saw a throne supported by angels. On it was a man with long hair and a beard. He smiled at me. Then we came back, but by a different way...When we were about to go out through the big door,....Our Lady said to me "You've seen this place? If everyone heard the word of God, this would be their kingdom." After that I came to myself.

Tarcisio has received several messages from Our Lady that have been published in a regular bulletin along with other news and other messages by the parish committee. Here are a few from the spring of 1986:

"Dear son, I've called you tonight because you should say this to the pilgrims: ''To fight against evil they must have an active conscience, they should read a passage from the gospel every morning and keep it in their minds and hearts and so overcome the trials that the day brings. (April 4, 1986)

"Most of those who come here come out of curiosity, and that's what saddens me the most; and that it's the young people who don't believe; they haven't understood that I've come to earth especially for them." [Tarcisio adds that she then blessed him in the name of the Holy Trinity.] (April 12, 1986)

Tarcisio writes that during an apparition Our Lady took his hand; he felt faint. She took him to a place of eternal silence and said to him, "See, my son, the people who are in purgatory are waiting to go up to heaven and see God; only your prayers can help them to attain that goal. Pray, pray, pray.'' (April 14, 1986)

He writes that on April 28, 1986, he was praying at the gate with his mother when suddenly Our Lady appeared to him and said, ''I'm happy because many pilgrims pray. My heart is full of sorrow for those who are still far from prayer.''

He saw Our Lady at the gate on May 7, 1986, and she said to him:

> ''Dear son, your prayer should not be only the rosary; your days should be a continuous prayer made up of good works, of love towards others, of penance; this is not just for you but for all who come to visit me. My son, when you recite the rosary, you should think that in each mystery there is contained all the love and suffering of my Son and of myself for all of you.''

In December 1988, Tarcisio began his obligatory two years of military service. In 1989, he was transferred from an army base near the French border to one at Brescia in northern Italy. His great desire is to be a paratrooper.

Mafalda

Mafalda Caputo lives with her husband Eliseo, an accountant, and their thirteen-year-old son, Vincenzo, in a small, tastefully furnished apartment near the prefabricated structure that serves as a church until the regular church is repaired. Their nineteen-year-old daughter Antonella lives at home when she is not away at school in Salerno. Vincenzo Caputo is one of the twelve boys who saw something at the castle gate on May 24, 1985.

Mafalda believed her son, Vincenzo, when he told her that he had seen Our Lady the night of May 24th, and she went to the little square every evening to say the rosary hoping that she would see Our Lady herself. One night in June 1985, she saw what she calls a sign, a light that came toward her from the far end of the walkway behind the gate of the castle and that disappeared when it reached the gate.

One night soon after Mafalda saw the light, she dreamed that she saw Our Lady. The dream was quite real, and it took away the anxiousness she had felt to have some kind of vision of the Blessed Virgin.

But then, on September 19, 1985, Mafalda did see Our Lady at the castle gate. "Little by little, an image of Our Lady took form, a light that grew larger and brighter and that opened up. When I saw the light I began to tremble." Mafalda could not see Our Lady clearly; she was blinded by so much light. Gradually the vision became clearer. Our Lady wore a grey gown and a black mantle. She had something in her hands, but Mafalda couldn't see it clearly, perhaps white flowers. That first time, Our Lady did not speak or give any message.

Again, on October 26, Mafalda saw Our Lady, this time dressed all in white, and with her hands joined in prayer and holding a rosary. "I was saying the rosary down there in the little square," Mafalda told Luciana. "The pastor was there; we were altogether there and Our Lady appeared to me." When she saw Our Lady, Mafalda began to tremble. Our Lady said to come to her, so Mafalda left the group standing around the microphone and went toward Our Lady. She found herself at the gate to the castle, stopped and knelt. Then, Mafalda states, "I asked her, 'Who are you?' Because the others had seen her with a blue mantle and with the Infant Jesus in her arms, and she answered me, 'I am the Virgin Immaculate Mother of God.' She had a voice, a voice, a marvelously musical voice, I can't explain it."

Luciana interviewed Mafalda. Here is an excerpt from the interview:

Luciana: Does Don Peppino [the pastor, Monsignor Giuseppe Amato] believe you?

Mafalda: Don Peppino didn't believe me at all at first.

He was that way with everybody at first. Even with me when Our Lady told me the first time, "I am the Immaculate Virgin Mother of Jesus," and I asked her then, "Aren't you Our Lady of the Castle?" She answered, "You call me that because I have appeared here, but I am the Immaculate Virgin Mother of Jesus." When I went to tell Don Peppino the first time that I heard Our Lady's voice, he said, "Thank you, Madam." Then when I received the messages, Our Lady said to me, "You should tell them to Don Peppino and he should tell them to the pilgrims." From then on, he began to act differently with me and with the others.

Luciana: The messages are given to the pilgrims through Don Peppino?

Mafalda: Yes, Don Peppino every evening says a message that Our Lady wants to be said to the pilgrims.

Luciana: What is this message? To pray?

Mafalda: No. To say to the pilgrims that, "When they come here to visit me and come up to the gate, even if they don't see me, I'm here." And he says that every evening he says it. The very first message that was given to me was for the people of Oliveto, that when they pray in the little square they should pray for the persons, for the people of this town. "Pray." And I asked her, "Why should we pray for these people?" And Our Lady answered, "Because they need it, pray for them." Having said that, she said, "Now I'll give you a message for the pilgrims; you tell the pastor, and the pastor will tell it to the pilgrims."

Luciana: Every evening he should repeat the same thing?

Mafalda: Every evening he should say it. Because about the pilgrims, Our Lady told me so many come, they come from all over.

Luciana: When was the last time you saw Our Lady?

Mafalda: November 2, and she said to me, ''You will not see me anymore,'' and I asked her why. She said that from now on I would not see her anymore and that I should become her missionary.

Luciana: Did Our Lady give you any particular message?

Mafalda: She said that I would not see her again and that I would carry her message to pray, and she told me that one day I would see her again but that it would be forever.

Luciana: Did you understand what she meant?

Mafalda: No. I told her, ''Your will be done.''

Luciana: What do you think she meant?

Mafalda: I think she meant two things, that now I'm being tried, and that I won't see her again until one day when I will see her again and then I'll see her always, or else I'll see her always when I die and go to heaven. She told me to pray for the leaders of nations, for the men who hold power in their hands, to pray for them, they don't pray. They have time only for preparing war and for dispersing violence in the world.

Luciana: You remember that message easily.

Mafalda: Yes, we with our prayers, we should pray so that they preach peace.

Luciana: That they preach peace is a hope of Our Lady's?

Mafalda: Yes.

Luciana: Was there any other particular message?

Mafalda: She told me that we should pray for our brothers and sisters who suffer from hunger. For those people, praying is not enough; also, we should help them out because they are our brothers and sisters who are suffering.

Mafalda has seen Our Lady three times at the castle gate. One of those times, October 29, 1985, Our Lady had the heavenly choir sing the hymn, "Queen of the Castle." That same evening the Blessed Virgin told Mafalda that she wanted a chapel. "Here I want a small chapel," she said, "to commemorate my appearances; and the feast in my honor should be celebrated on May 24, the day of Saint Macarius."

Since November 2 when Mary told her there would be no more visions, Mafalda hears Our Lady's voice. We asked her if the voice comes from inside her, a voice in her heart or in her mind. She said that she hears Our Lady's voice the same way she hears mine. It comes from outside her from an indeterminate direction. She hears the voice with her ears.

On December 15, at 1:30 in the morning, a voice woke Mafalda calling her name. Her son Vincenzo woke up and said, "Mother, they're calling you." She opened her eyes and saw a light in the general shape of a human form. The voice, Mafalda recognized it as Our Lady's, said, "You're tired, but you have to get up; get up."

Our Lady then told Mafalda that no one on earth should ever be without a family, because each person has a Father in heaven who is God, and a mother in heaven who is not only Jesus' mother but also the mother of each one of us.

On January 10, 1986, Our Lady gave Mafalda a message for all humanity. This message, with some revisions, was printed and distributed to whoever came to the little square in Oliveto Citra in January and early February 1986. Here is the complete text, without any revision, as Mafalda says Our Lady dictated it to her:

Message of the Immaculate Virgin Mother of Jesus, message for all mankind. Write this down, my

51

daughter.

My dear children, God sends me on earth to come to save all because the whole world is in danger. I come among you to bring peace to your hearts. God wants that peace to reign in the hearts of all mankind, and he wants the conversion of all peoples.

Therefore, my dear children, pray, pray, pray; if you do not pray, you will receive nothing.

The time that you have left is short; there will be earthquakes, disasters, and famines for the inhabitants of the earth.

Dear children, when God comes among you with some manifestation, he does not come as a joke. He does not joke, and he is not afraid of men, so take this message seriously.

I will pray that God will not punish you. God says, *Save yourselves, pray much, and do penance, and be converted, with prayer you can obtain everything. People should not bow only before God, but also toward their own brothers and sisters who suffer fighting hunger in the world.*

Mankind is full of serious sins that offend the love of God.

Peace on earth is about to end, the world cannot be saved without peace, but the world will find peace only if mankind returns to God. My children, I beg you to pray for the conversion of all peoples; do penance and save yourselves from hell. I will engage in the final struggle against Satan which will conclude with the triumph of my Immaculate Heart and with the coming of the kingdom of God in the world.

Those who refuse God today will go far from him tomorrow into hell. I have presented myself to you as the Immaculate Virgin Mother of Jesus, and I come to bring to you, dear children, mercy, forgiveness, and peace in the name of God the Father.

Have this message read to priests, and I want it to be communicated to everyone as soon as possible.

Do not be ashamed of my message, but say it to everyone you meet. For the spreading of my message is a great apostolic work, because with information about the apparitions and with knowledge of the messages, many people will pray more.

Now my children I bless you all.

Remember: Prayer and penance, and pray for the conversion of all mankind.

Our Lady dictated to Mafalda, at 10:00 p.m. on February 11, 1986, a message for the people of Oliveto Citra.

My dear children, I invite you to pray much in these days because Satan has made himself evident in a particular way in this town. So pray, pray, pray so that all I have planned may come about. That way, Satan can't do anything.

Frequently, Our Lady gives Mafalda messages for everyone. The parish committee regularly prints and distributes these messages. Here is a message of April 1986. Mafalda wrote:

I asked Our Lady if there is danger of a third world war. Our Lady answered me with this message:

"Dear children, do not ask, but be converted, and pray much. I, Mary, will not leave you, but I want you to understand once and for all that the world is at the edge of the abyss.

Mankind is sliding toward a frightening precipice; therefore, my children, pray, pray, pray; be converted and do penance. The three-fold way to save yourselves from sin and punishment is: prayer, conversion, and penance.

And all this can go toward saving the world from a Third World War.

I, Mary, Mother of God, invite all of you to love God and also your brothers and sisters. I bless you in the name of the Most Holy Trinity.

Mafalda Caputo is a neat and attractive woman in her forties, clearly a good wife and mother, and a good housekeeper. She prays much, several hours a day, says the rosary, goes to daily Mass.

Mafalda has taken to heart what she considers a commission from Our Lady to act as an apostle. In the evening she goes to the small square and talks to the pilgrims, telling them about Our Lady and about the apparitions and the messages.

Others Who See Our Lady

There are several other people living at Oliveto Citra who see Our Lady and who receive messages from her. Antonia Ianecce, eleven years old, a friend of Marco De Bellis and in school with him, quite timid, speaks very little. She often has ecstasies in which she sees Mary or Jesus and speaks with them. Our Lady has given her many messages, for herself, for her family, and regarding the whole world.

Antonia began, sometimes, to hear a choir sing the hymn, "Our Lady of the Castle," in the fall of 1985. Later, she began, sometimes, to hear Our Lady speak to her. A little less than a year later, Our Lady began to appear to her and to speak to her. For example, on Antonia's birthday, May 3, 1987, Our Lady appeared and said to her, "Antonia, you were born on a good day because you were born in my month. I am the Immaculate Virgin without original stain. I am the mama of Jesus and of all children, and of all mothers. And I am Our Lady of the Roses." A short time later, she appeared again and repeated that she is the Immaculate Virgin, the mother of Jesus and of all children and mothers, and Our Lady of the Roses.

In early June 1987, Our Lady appeared to Antonia and

told her, "Something beautiful will happen to you tonight." That night Jesus, dressed all in white, appeared to Antonia and gave her the gift of the Holy Spirit.

At the time of this writing, Antonia has received several secrets: six for the world, four for her family, and ten secrets about her own future. She will not reveal any of them.

Giovanna Coglianese, eighty-six years old, has lived in Oliveto Citra all her life. She helps out in the rectory as assistant housekeeper for Monsignor Amato. She sees Mary with increasing frequency, several times a month now, usually at the gate of the castle, but sometimes in the rectory.

Of the twelve boys who first saw Mary on May 24, 1985, only Mimmo De Guidis still sees her fairly often. The twins, Carmine and Dino Acquaviva, see Our Lady two or three times a year.

All those who see Our Lady regularly fast on Friday and say the rosary every day. Most of them meet every Saturday to pray together and to receive instructions in the spiritual life, especially on personal prayer.

CHAPTER 6

THE PARISH PRIEST

Oliveto Citra lies in the diocese of Campagna. Several years ago the Campagna diocese was put directly under the head of the Archdiocese of Salerno, Archbishop Guerino Grimaldi, who is therefore also the Bishop of Campagna. For ordinary administration, however, the diocese of Campagna has its own vicar general, Monsignor Giuseppe Amato, the pastor of the parish of Oliveto Citra. Everyone in Oliveto Citra knows him as Don Peppino.

Don Peppino

The events at Oliveto Citra in many ways center on Monsignor Amato, or Don Peppino. The persons who see Our Lady frequently have little contact with one another apart from their weekly meeting. They have, in fact, almost nothing in common except their extraordinary contacts with Our Lady. But they all refer what they see and hear to Don Peppino. He keeps the records, the signed testimonies, and any other documents. He is, to one degree or another, their spiritual director. They all love him and trust him.

Don Peppino is not just an ordinary parish priest. As vicar general of a diocese, he carries many of the responsibilities of a bishop. He is slow to speak and to act, wise, prudent, and warmly affable. He radiates common sense, good judgment, dependability and strength of character. He loves his people and takes responsibility for pastoring them.

What does he think about the apparitions? At first quite skeptical, Don Peppino soon took into account the spiritual fruits of what was happening—the conversion, the increased attendance at Sunday Mass, the whole new spirit in his parish. He knows that the same credibility cannot be given to everything that goes on in his parish. Not everyone who says, ''I have seen Our Lady'' has necessarily really seen her.

But it is quite clear to the pastor that Our Lady has come to Oliveto Citra in a new and extraordinary way, that she has made herself seen and heard in his parish and especially at the gate of the castle many times and to many different people. And that what Our Lady says and does in his parish has meaning for the world outside Oliveto Citra, for the whole Church, and for all mankind.

We have spoken with Don Peppino many times. He speaks calmly, openly, and frankly, and he stresses the spiritual aspects of the apparitions and their consequences. The media, he says, especially newspapers and magazines in Italy, have often distorted the meaning and the message of the apparitions of Our Lady here. Media coverage cannot explain the great numbers of pilgrims that come to the castle gate in the little square. We have to ask ourselves why do people come here? Why do we find license plates from all over Italy on cars and buses parked near the little square, and people coming here from all over the world? Why are so many people converted here, helped spiritually, brought closer to the Church and to God? They do not come because of the media coverage. And the help they receive seems to be both substantial and lasting in many cases.

What he finds special about the apparitions here is that in the past in other parts of the world, Our Lady has appeared several times to one or to a few people. But here she has already appeared hundreds, even thousands of times to hundreds of people. This has never happened before in the history of Marian apparitions.

Our Lady, and Don Peppino underlines the fact, calls us to prayer. She calls us urgently and sincerely. She is displeased when the rosary is said poorly. She wants us to pray the rosary, and to pray it fervently, prayerfully.

She calls us to pray for the world, for sinners, for peace. She calls the people here to pray not only for the people of Oliveto Citra because they need conversion so badly, but for all mankind. She speaks and acts repeatedly and insistently because the world has lost its sense of the spiritual. Our Lady wants to build a new people and a new Church.

The Church and Oliveto Citra

What is the stance of the official Church regarding the events at Oliveto Citra? At the local level, Don Peppino himself represents the Church. And he evaluates the apparitions and their results prudently but quite positively.

I visited Archbishop Guerino Grimaldi of Salerno on April 19, 1986. A solidly-built, burly man about sixty-five years old, with heavy neck and shoulders and a determined manner that suits his strong face and grey crew-cut, he spoke bluntly although rarely looking at me. The Archbishop was quite skeptical about the apparitions at Oliveto Citra. He claimed to find no positive elements in the events there, other than that people come together to pray. And he finds considerable confusion among various people who say they have had visions of Our Lady. However, he himself had not been to Oliveto Citra since the apparitions began, nor had he spoken personally with people who say they have seen Our Lady.

The Archbishop of Salerno appointed a diocesan commission to look into the matter and to make a preliminary judgment, either positive or negative. The commission consisted of four persons: the vicar general of the Archdiocese of Salerno, Monsignor Francesco Spaduzzi; a Salerno theology teacher, Rev. Michele De Rosa; the Contursi Terme parish priest, Monsignor Salvatore Ciani; a lay deacon and retired high school principal, Mr. Attilio Punzi. By late April 1986, they had taped interviews with about sixty persons, although Don Peppino knew of only about ten such interviews. The other fifty people interviewed were apparently chosen at random by the commission. After analyzing the tapes, the commission wrote a report and turned it in to the Archbishop. This report has not been made public nor has the Archbishop stated any preliminary judgment as to the general authenticity of the apparitions at Oliveto Citra. Ordinarily, according to standard procedure, the Archbishop would have made a preliminary statement after an initial brief investigation. For example, he could have said that the alleged appearances of Our Lady appear to have no basis in reality. Or he could have designated Oliveto Citra as a proper place for devotion to Mary; this would have been the normal form for a beginning and tentative approval on the part of the Archbishop. However, strangely, none of this has happened even after almost four years. And no official statement is anticipated.

There are rumors that the diocesan commission's report to the Archbishop was negative, that it said, "There are not sufficient reasons to affirm that Our Lady appears at Oliveto Citra." At any rate, the commission has finished its work and apparently considers the case closed.

In October 1987, Monsignor Francesco Spaduzzi wrote in the official archdiocesan bulletin for the clergy about the alleged apparitions at Oliveto Citra and set down certain directives. The archdiocesan vicar general quotes an alleged message of Mary: "Participate in the Mass because Jesus is alive and truly present in the tabernacle waiting to fill your hearts with grace." Although this is the only message he quotes, he excoriates its theology as a throwback to the Middle Ages. He goes on to question the character of some who say they have seen Our Lady, accusing two of them of telling lies.

He quite falsely claims that an earlier version of this book, in Italian, by Robert Faricy, anticipates a positive judgment from Archbishop Grimaldi regarding the events at Oliveto Citra. On the contrary, the Italian version of the book, like this one, describes the negative attitude of the Archbishop and anticipates nothing. In fact, it seems possible that no judgment will be forthcoming from the Archbishop for some time at least.

Monsignor Spaduzzi forbids priests and religious to organize or accompany pilgrimages to Oliveto Citra; he forbids Mass outdoors without permission of the Archbishop; he forbids priests and religious to be members of the parish committee; he repeats Church teaching on exorcisms. He states that the faithful go to Oliveto at their own spiritual risk, and he recommends prudence in matters regarding apparitions.

Later, in a television interview, Monsignor Spaduzzi declared that, ''You cannot say that everything is negative at Oliveto Citra.'' As Monsignor Amato has written in a letter to an Italian magazine in June 1987, ''facing the events at Oliveto Citra, the Church is neither gullible nor disrespectful; it remains in an attitude of waiting.''

The Vatican follows what is happening at Oliveto Citra through the special section for apparitions that exists in the Sacred Congregation for the Doctrine of the Faith. The Vatican will not, of course, intervene as long as it sees that the matter is handled adequately at the local level.

In any case, it could be a long time before any definitive Church approval or disapproval might be announced. In the meantime, everyone is free to accept or not accept the apparitions as valid. As long as the Church makes no statement, each of us is free to believe or not to believe in the authenticity of the events at Oliveto Citra.

The Castle Gate

The Castle

Monsignor Guseppe Amato at the blessing of the little chapel with the statue of Our Lady.

A crowd on the stairway to the Castle gate and in the small squar

Anita Rio with her daughter Sara

Carmine Acquaviva

Dino Acquaviva

Umberto Gaghardi

Mafalda Caputo

Antonella Giordano

Tarcisio Biasi

The gate to the Castle and the small chapel

Ana and Sabrina DeBellis

Donato Bracigliano

Marco DeBellis

Giovanna Coglianese

Antonia Iannece while seeing Our Lady.

Luciana Pecaraio, Fr. Robert Faricy and Filomena Palmieri

The alley just beyond the gate where Our Lady appears

CHAPTER 7

SIGNS AND WONDERS

A number of extraordinary events, some testified to by large numbers of people, have taken place at Oliveto Citra since the first apparition on May 24, 1985. These include strange phenomena in the sky, unusual behavior of the sun, healings, and visions. This chapter reports some of these things.

Signs in the Sky

On July 20, 1985, at about 10:30 p.m., all who were present in the little square, and many persons in other parts of the town and outside it, saw a cloud of an intense red color form over the castle and circle the square. Several people fainted. Signed testimonies are in the parish rectory. Over fifty people claim to have seen Our Lady at the castle gate while the cloud was circling.

Several people have claimed to have seen the sun change color. For example, signed statements from members of a pilgrimage from Palermo testify that on November 24, 1985, many people saw, from the bus leaving Oliveto Citra for Palermo, the sun turn white and then green surrounded by purple and other colors. On November 30, 1985, about twenty people signed a statement that on the afternoon of that day they saw the sun change color. They also saw fifty-nine birds in formation spelling out the letters A and V and E to spell ave, the first word of the Latin version of the "Hail Mary."

Seven people signed statements that they saw a luminous object like a dove flying over the castle on December 19, 1985. Two other persons saw a shiny dove over the castle some days later, one on December 23 and the other on December 30. Almost all present saw the sun pulsate and "dance" at the official blessing of the tiny chapel at the castle gate in April 1987. The videotape of this phenomenon is in the possession of the parish committee.

Anna's Letter

Of all the mysterious signs at the gate to the castle, probably the strangest is that of the letter that disappeared. Signed statements by Anna D'Antuono and Lucia D'Aniello, both from the town of Sant'Antonio Abate, testify to what happened.

Anna, a seven-year-old girl, had written a letter to Jesus before she left her house to come with the pilgrimage to Oliveto Citra. The letter said, "Dear Baby Jesus, I want to have you in my little bed so that I can stand and look at you and be happy, happy." On December 16, 1985, Anna took the letter to the gate, handed it to an adult, Anna Maria Siano-Mercurio of Sant'Antonio Abate, who in turn handed it to another adult, Lucia D'Aniello, who tossed the letter over the gate. Anna claims that at that instant she saw a normal-looking hand, not apparently attached to a body, reach out of nowhere and take the letter. At any rate, all testify that the letter disappeared from sight.

After a few minutes, at the suggestion of Father Giacomo Selvi, a parish priest from the town of Agropoli, Lucia D'Aniello went back to the gate to see if the letter had really disappeared. She could not find the letter. Instead, Our

Lady appeared to her and said, "I have taken the letter. Take this message to the people: I can no longer hold back the righteous arm of my Son; be converted, and especially the men."

Healings

Rocco Romano, an engineer from Frattamaggiore, near Naples, in a statement dated November 9, 1985, testifies to the healing of his eyes:

> For some months I had known through my friend Raffaele Del Prete of Frattamaggiore that there were apparitions of Our Lady in Oliveto Citra. I went several times to the place of the apparitions with a spirit not so much critical as skeptical.

On September 12, Mr. Romano said a short prayer to Our Lady of Oliveto Citra asking to be healed of an eye disease. He had been diagnosed as having diabetic retinopathy of the first and second stages. On September 15, Mr. Romano had an eye examination by Dr. Testa, Professor at the University of Naples, who found no evidence of any disease.

On September 12, the day that Rocco Romano said the prayer for healing to our Lady of Oliveto Citra, his friend Rafaele Del Prete was in Oliveto Citra. Del Prete knew nothing of Romano's eye disease. At the castle gate he received a message: "When you return to Fratta, tell Rocco Romano that what he asked for has already been given to him, and that he should come and thank me." He was puzzled until he met Rocco Romano on the afternoon of September 15, and Romano explained what had happened. Copies of signed statements and of the diagnosis are in the parish rectory.

Rita Salvatore was diagnosed July 14, 1986 by Dr. Francesco Lanzillo, a gynecologist of Frattamaggiore near Naples, as having an ovarian cyst. Rita prayed at the castle gate to be healed. An examination on September 5, 1986, showed the cyst reduced in size; and on May 18, 1987, Dr. Lanzillo could find no evidence of the cyst.

Raffaele Barnes received a severe concussion, a fractured jaw, and a badly broken left leg in an automobile accident in Naples on September 21, 1986. He asked for prayers for healing to Our Lady of the Castle; a Naples prayer group and one of the people who see Our Lady at Oliveto Citra prayed for him. And he prayed himself to Our Lady, Queen of the Castle. His condition became much better almost immediately; planned surgery was canceled, and no further treatment was necessary other than a brace on his fractured jaw. On November 12, the Cardelli Hospital in Naples declared him healed.

A seven-year-old boy of Naples, Salvatore Grillo, was diagnosed on February 26, 1986, as almost completely deaf. His mother, having heard about the apparitions at Oliveto Citra, prayed to Our Lady of the Castle that Salvatore's hearing would return. On March 6, 1986, Dr. Elio Marciano of the University of Naples declared that Salvatore should not wear his two hearing aids anymore because his hearing was perfectly normal.

Salvatore Giuri of Lecce in southeastern Italy left his orthopedic back brace at the castle gate on August 30, 1987. Giuri had suffered severe pain since 1978 because of a herniated disk. Surgery, physiotherapy, and laser therapy all proved ineffective. Microsurgery was decided against as being too risky for the little promise it held of healing. Acupuncture provided only minimal relief. On Saturday, July 18, 1987, Giuri prayed for healing of his back at the castle gate at Oliveto Citra. He returned to Lecce during the night and, completely healed, played soccer on Sunday morning. A quite lengthy documentation is in the office of the parish committee.

Allergic to antibiotics, Paulette Jaffre of Miano, near Naples, was unable to follow the normal treatment of her throat ulcers. Unable to swallow, she had already lost over fifty pounds in a few months when, late in 1986, she returned to her native France for treatment. She could eat only with pain and had lost all taste and smell. The treatment, however, did not help since she could not take antibiotics of any kind. In May 1987, Paulette came back to Italy and visited Oliveto Citra several times. One evening at the end of May, on one of those visits, praying at the castle gates, she began to cry. She found, to her surprise, that she could taste the salt of her tears. Then she smelled a strong and extraordinary perfume of flowers. She and her husband remained, praying, until two the next morning. When she awoke after a night's sleep, she could swallow her saliva without any discomfort. She was completely healed. During the summer when she returned to her doctor in France, he confirmed the healing.

The testimony of Liliana Iselle Vangelisti, of Bolzano in northern Italy, resembles the healing of the woman who suffered from a hemorrhage (Matthew 9:20-22). She writes:

Here is what happened. For seventeen or eighteen years the fact of being a woman had become for me a heavy reality that forced me, almost every month, to stay in bed for several days in order to avoid the danger of bad hemorrhage. In spite of medicine and bed-rest, I often still hemorrhaged.

Her condition interfered with her work as a teacher, and caused her anxiety and serious worry. The doctors felt that surgery, overall, might well make things worse.

Liliana continues:

...During Easter vacation of 1987, out of love for Our Lady, to pay her a courtesy visit, I went to Oliveto Citra near Salerno. I went with much faith, and with much love, believing in the apparitions there.

There, I met one of the people who sees Our Lady, Umberto Gagliardi, with whom I spoke. I asked him what happens when he sees her. I was really moved when he told me that before leaving him, she sometimes takes his hand.

This contact with Our Lady seemed marvelous to me, something outstanding. Well, the next evening I went to pray at the gate and I found Umberto Gagliardi there kneeling in prayer. He recognized me and said hello, and a little later he showed me, pointing, where he had just seen Our Lady. She was there, next to the gate, inside it, near the fig tree on the right. I didn't see her, but I firmly believed she was there.

I saw Umberto go back to seeing Our Lady. At a certain moment he. . .told me and a blond girl, just out of the hospital after serious surgery, to put our hands on the gate. After a little while I saw him follow with his eyes and head a movement. Our Lady came to us to touch our hands and to hold them in hers (I learned this later). In that moment I felt within me, in my heart, something indescribable, so much joy, peace, and an interior revelation what mercy really is. . .

From that April 1987 until now (February 1988), I have had no hemorrhages, although my regular cycle has continued. Our Lady has restored to me. . .my freedom and my serenity.

These and other healings are documented medically; the documentation can be found in the parish committee office.

But besides physical healings, the most numerous and many of the most dramatic healings at Oliveto Citra have been spiritual, moral, and psychological. A quite large number of young people addicted to drugs have been completely cured. Many marriages have been healed. And, especially, there have been innumerable conversions.

Other Testimonies

Several signed statements refer to smelling an unusual perfume, unlike any other. Many people who claim to have seen Our Lady, and many who do not, have smelled this perfume.

Many have signed statements saying they have seen a light, or bright lights, or a light in the form of a human figure. Others who have spoken to us have said they have seen lights or luminous shapes, even though they never reported it to the parish committee or to Monsignor Amato, the parish priest.

What is most striking about the documentation in the parish committee office is the large number of signed declarations of persons who claim to have seen Our Lady. Many of these also say they heard her speak, and have recorded on paper what she reportedly said. Many of these declarations are from pilgrims from all over Italy, mostly from the southern half of the Italian peninsula. It would be almost impossible and probably not very profitable to try to verify all or even most of them.

Just for December 1985, a month when the cold weather and the wind through the little square keep many pilgrims from coming to Oliveto Citra, a month of relatively few people at the gate in the evening, there are over one hundred sworn statements of persons who say they have seen Our Lady. Here are a few of them, taken at random:

> I, the undersigned, Lucia T., born at C. on May 20, 1965, living at . . ., declare that on December 16, 1985, at 11:40 p.m., at Oliveto Citra, at the gate to the castle, I saw an image of Our Lady dressed in white at the end of the walkway, and she was smiling.

> [signed] Lucia T.

> I, the undersigned, Rita R., born at B. on October 8, 1977, and residing at . . ., declare that on Sunday, December 8, 1985, I saw Our Lady . . . She was dressed in a rose-colored dress with a white mantle. She told me to tell others that the rosary should be said in every home, and that she wished she could embrace every-

one present, but she has only two arms. Right after that she came toward me with the Baby Jesus in her arm and she put him in my arms...

[signed] Rita R.

On December 17, Adriana F. of B. saw our Lady and received this message from her:

People are shipwrecked in their faith. They do not have the courage to do the right thing. I have come to help them to be converted and therefore to turn to God; that is, to faith in God and to works of charity and to devout participation in the Mass.''

Our Lady also gave her some secrets:

I was in prayer with my eyes closed, and I felt that Our Lady was among us. In particular, I saw a white light high up at the castle, above the gate. And inside the gate I saw the figure of the Virgin with the child in her arm. She repeated over and over that we should all pray, pray, pray, and she invited us not to lose hope, and to trust in her loving love.

December 19, 1985

I, the undersigned, Alfonsina P., born March 23, 1930, at P., now residing at..., declare that in front of the front gate of the castle of Oliveto Citra at about five p.m.,...I saw Our Lady. Her dress was blue. She had the Baby Jesus supported by her arm, while in her left arm she held a bouquet of flowers. At a certain point the Virgin said to me, ''All will go well for you. Have your son come so that for him too everything will go well. They do not believe that you see me, but you should speak up loudly that you see me, because I will make myself seen also by others. The apparition lasted about thirty minutes.

Oliveto Citra,
December 22, 1985.
[signed] Vincenzo P.

There is a note that Alfonsina P. is illiterate, and that the above was written at her dictation.

I, the undersigned, Pepe C., born June 27, 1962, at P., living at..., declare that on December 22, 1985, I saw Our Lady in a luminous cloud...And I saw the same vision on December 25. She had the infant in her arms, and a rosary hung from his little hands. She was dressed in white with a sky-blue mantle. She gave me a message which goes like this: "It is necessary to pray; it is necessary to pray; it is necessary to pray. Leave ugly things. Don't do any more evil. Do penance..."

> Oliveto Citra,
> December 25, 1985
> [signed] Pepe C.

Comments on the Visions

The pastor, Monsignor Amato, points out that the vast majority of those who say they have seen the Blessed Virgin do not claim to have received any message. Most only see the figure of Our Lady, usually dressed in white with a blue mantle, often smiling. Few receive messages. And Don Peppino makes these wise comments:

> Different people react differently to having visions. In some, the vision results in an immediate and sincere conversion. In others it results in a gradual return to God and to the Christian life. And finally in others the results touch the limits of the absurd in this sense: either they reject the gift because they are blocked by human respect, or they do not accept it because they do not want to change their lives and be converted.

Don Peppino finds a common thread in the messages that Our Lady gives to people at Oliveto Citra. Above all, there is an urgent call to pray. And there is an invitation to penance expressed in concrete ways: fasting and works of charity. And there is a strong call to conversion. Prayer, penance, conversion. This is what Our Lady at Oliveto Citra calls us to. And when Mary warns us about divine punishments in the form of disasters, famines, earthquakes, these messages are messages of hope and encouragement to pray and to do penance. These catastrophes can be averted by prayer and penance.

CHAPTER 8

THE NEWNESS OF OLIVETO CITRA

Oliveto Citra has become a place of pilgrimage. It seems certain that more and more pilgrims will come despite the total lack of hotels or other housing because what happens at the castle gate in the little square is unique, new in the history of pilgrimages.

What is Different About Oliveto Citra?

Pilgrims come to a place where Our Lady has appeared and spoken, to where she appears and speaks daily to several people. Many pilgrims see and hear her themselves.

Not all pilgrims see Our Lady. Not even most of them. But hundreds of pilgrims have stated that Mary has appeared to them at the castle gate. Many have said it in tears, shaken, profoundly moved. And some have written signed accounts of their experiences and left them with the parish committee for the apparitions.

What kind of pilgrims see Our Lady? What kind of people can expect to see her? I can find no criterion, no common denominator, no significant statistic that would point to a certain type of person as a likely candidate to see the Blessed Virgin Mary.

Salvatore M. from Catania in Sicily saw her at the gate; he carries the stigmata, the five wounds of Jesus crucified, in his body, and he is generally recognized as a holy person. Umberto Gagliardi sees Our Lady often; when he first saw her he was a non-practicing Catholic. Many people who are outstanding Christians and who might be said to have a certain holiness do not see her. And many who do not practice their religion to any great extent and whose faith at best is lukewarm do see her. Holiness or the lack of it does not seem to be a criterion.

Nor does age. Marco De Bellis is only eleven years old. Giovanna Coglianese is over eighty. Those who see her have all degrees of education, culture, intelligence. We can find no criterion, no common cluster of qualities among those who see Our Lady at the gate.

This situation, where anyone might have a vision of the Blessed Virgin Mary, presents certain obvious difficulties. For one thing, it could seem to cheapen somehow Marian apparitions. Wholesale apparitions of Our Lady might seem less important, somehow cheap.

Secondly, the situation at Oliveto Citra could encourage people to attach more importance to special religious experiences than is healthy. People could become more attached to having a vision than to God. They could thirst unhealthily for exotic experiences and for special treatment from God, and then be unhealthily downcast when they find themselves not singled out for special treatment.

These problems are real. This is why, surely, Our Lady has instructed Father Amato, through Mafalda, to tell the crowd in the little square, night after night, not to be disappointed or feel bad if they do not see Our Lady. She is present to them, and that is what is important.

Furthermore, there is an important message in the extraordinary fact of so many people seeing Our Lady so often. The numbers of people and the frequency convey strongly an urgency on the part of Our Lady, even a kind of desperation. She is begging us to listen. She is going to extremes so that we hear her. She resorts to unusual and even unprecedented behavior so that we will take notice, repent, be converted, believe—so that we will listen to her with our hearts.

Oliveto Citra and Medjugorje

Since June of 1981, Our Lady has appeared daily to a small group of young people in the village of Medjugorje, a Croatian parish in Herzegovina, Yugoslavia. There are some differences and some similarities between Oliveto Citra and Medjugorje.

The biggest difference is that the Medjugorje apparitions are to a small, regular group of young people, six in the beginning and now four. They occur every evening at the same hour, 5:40 p.m. They are regular, predictable, and to a fixed group. The apparitions at Oliveto Citra, on the other hand, are to hundreds of people, at any time although especially in the evening and at night, with no predictability or regularity. Even those who often see Our Lady do not form a group, hardly knew one another before the apparitions began, and do not even all live in Oliveto Citra.

What are the likenesses between Oliveto Citra and Medjugorje? In particular, the messages are similar. The message of both Oliveto Citra and Medjugorje is: pray, pray, pray. Our Lady calls us to pray: to pray for sinners, to pray for conversions, to pray for the world, to pray for peace. In both cases, Our Lady urges us to say the rosary daily, all fifteen mysteries. And, both at Medjugorje and at Oliveto Citra, Our Lady calls us to do penance, to fast on Fridays.

And there appear some quite striking particular coincidences. In the early summer of 1985, Our Lady told the young people at Medjugorje that her birthday was August 5. This was not widely known and, as far as we know, remains unpublished and unpromulgated. On August 5,

1985, Our Lady appeared at the castle gate to Anita Rio and told her, "It's my birthday." The same day, and quite independently, she appeared to Umberto Gagliardi and told him, too, that it was her birthday. And she may well have told others. Regarding August 5 as Our Lady's birthday, I find no evidence of any influence on either Anita and Umberto coming from Medjugorje. The Medjugorje birth date revelation and the Oliveto Citra revelations of the same date appear to be quite independent.

Many people at Medjugorje have, on frequent occasions, seen the sun move oddly and change color. People at Oliveto, although fewer and less often, have also seen the sun behave strangely and turn various colors. Both Medjugorje and Oliveto Citra have witnessed numerous conversions and some remarkable healings.

All things considered, however, Oliveto Citra stands alone and unprecedented as the story of a mother who urgently, and even desperately, cries out to her children urging them to pray, warning them, loving them and wanting to save them. And, in her urgency and near desperation, in her fierce maternal love, takes extreme measures and goes well beyond the boundaries of all her previous apparitions.

CHAPTER 9

EVALUATION

How does the Church evaluate a situation like that of Oliveto Citra? What procedure does the Church follow to assess the validity of apparitions? In this chapter, we want to describe briefly the Church's procedure and its criteria for evaluating apparitions like those currently at Oliveto Citra. We want to apply the criteria to Oliveto Citra in an informal and preliminary way so as to offer to the reader the possibility of evaluating events there by using the same general criteria that the Church uses.

In an unpublished and generally unavailable document, the Sacred Congregation for the Doctrine of the Faith, in the Vatican, sets forth the procedure and the criteria for making official judgments about contemporary apparitions. The title of the document is *Norms of the Sacred Congregation for the Doctrine of the Faith about How to Proceed in Judging Alleged Apparitions and Revelations*. It is written in Latin.

This document is sent by the Holy See, from the Sacred Congregation for the Doctrine of the Faith, now headed by Cardinal Joseph Ratzinger, to the bishop of any diocese in which alleged apparitions take place. When the local bishop investigates the alleged apparitions, either personally or through a representative or by means of a specially named diocesan commission, he is supposed to follow the procedure and the criteria laid down in the Vatican document.

The document begins by pointing out that today the mass media promulgate rapidly information about alleged apparitions. And, because of the ease of travel in these times, pilgrims can visit places of alleged apparitions with relatively little difficulty. At the same time, it is not at all easy for Church authorities to arrive with due speed at a judgment about the authenticity of such apparitions. Therefore, the Holy See, in order to help local bishops as well as national conferences of bishops, states some norms for action and some criteria of judgment.

Norms for action. The local Church authorities, the document says, are to follow a three-step procedure. 1) They should make a preliminary judgment of the facts in the case according to criteria set down later in the document. 2) If this preliminary judgment is favorable, they should permit public manifestations of devotion and worship, prudently letting it be known that for the time being at least no obstacle prevents such public devotions and worship regarding the alleged apparitions. 3) After a certain time has elapsed, and in the light of experience — especially of spiritual fruit and of new devotion — a judgment of truth and of heavenly origin can be made if the case warrants such a judgment.

The Vatican document further states that local Church authorities have a grave responsibility to keep informed and to watch over what goes on. They can even promote new devotions and ways of worshipping that have arisen in the context of the alleged apparitions. And they should intervene to correct abuses or any doctrinal error and guard against false mysticism.

''Local authorities'' of course, means the local bishop, in the case of Oliveta Citra, the Archbishop of Salerno. He can, if he so wishes, refer the matter to regional or national bishops' conferences, or even to the Holy See.

Criteria for evaluation. What are the criteria, according to the Holy See, for evaluating alleged apparitions? And how do they apply to the apparitions at Oliveto Citra?

Here are the negative criteria, things which would indicate that apparitions might be false:

First, obvious error, either about the facts, or in doctrine;

Secondly, if commercial endeavor, money-making (*lucro*) has an important role with regard to the apparitions;

Thirdly, gravely immoral acts on the part of the principal persons involved in the apparitions, or any mental illness on their part, or evidence of collective hysteria.

How do these negative criteria apply to Oliveto Citra?

First of all, we have found no error regarding the basic facts and no error of doctrine. Secondly, there is no evidence of any commercialism or effort to "make money." Rosaries, medals, or other religious objects are not sold. No collections are taken up at the castle gate. No hotels or boarding houses have sprung up to accommodate the pilgrims. No one at Oliveto Citra seems to be making any money at all from the daily influx of pilgrims.

Furthermore, in speaking with those people who are, at least at present, the persons who seem to have important roles in the apparitions, and who are referred to in the previous chapters, we have found no evidence at all of serious sinfulness or of any kind of psychological aberrance. On the other hand, it seems quite possible that one or more of the hundreds of people who think or say that they have seen Our Lady, or have heard her, or have seen visions of some kind, may well live a gravely sinful life or have some kind of mental illness or be in doctrinal error or have attributed, through ignorance or misunderstanding, doctrinal error to God, or to Mary, or to the saints.

Somewhere, the line has to be drawn between those who have the main roles in seeing Our Lady and those who have relatively small or peripheral roles. The criteria to investigate seriously, it seems to us, must be applied to the principal persons. It would be nearly impossible to investigate seriously how the criteria fit everyone who claims visions or locutions; nor does it seem at all necessary or appropriate.

What about the possibility of mass hysteria? Apart from the inevitable presence of some people with hysterical tendencies, could the crowds of people in the little square every evening be somehow victims of mass hysteria in such a way that some would think they had visions? The possibility can be easily eliminated. We have occasionally seen somewhat hysterical persons at the castle gate. I (Robert Faricy) once saw a woman weep and scream when a small cloud rose over the castle, and I have seen two men get excited about a shadow on a wall. But we have seen no evidence of any mass hysteria. On the contrary, the prayers, hymns, and rosary are conducted by the parish committee and under the direct supervision of Monsignor Amato in such a way as to preclude any hysterical climate.

The positive criteria for judging the authenticity of alleged apparitions are:

First, moral certitude or at least high probability that the facts are as claimed;

Secondly, particular circumstances. The persons having the apparitions must be judged as having good morals, psychological balance, sincerity, and respect for Church authority. In the case of Oliveta Citra, the main persons involved in the apparitions, those people whom we refer to in the preceding chapters, all exhibit good morals, psychological health, sincerity, and a love for the Church, as well as respect for Church authority. We do not think it appropriate to try to ascertain the morals and psychological balance and other qualities of everyone who claims visions.

A further positive criterion, the theological and spiritual doctrine involved must be free from error. This certainly seems to be true at Oliveto Citra. There is no evidence either of false doctrine or of any kind of exaggeration in the spirituality there.

Finally, the document from the Holy See gives as positive signs, spiritual fruits and healthy religious devotion. As examples, it names a strong spirit of prayer, and conversions. There can be no doubt about the spiritual fruits of the events at Oliveto Citra. The spirit of prayer is manifest every evening in the little square in front of the castle gate. Conversions are numerous, both of residents of Oliveto Citra and of those who come from outside the town. The number of people in Oliveto Citra who go to Mass and who receive the sacraments regularly has greatly increased.

Conclusion

The apparitions at Oliveto Citra show no signs of ending or even of decreasing in frequency. The number of pilgrims can be expected to keep increasing for some time. It seems much too early for any definitive judgment about what is happening at Oliveto Citra.

As the same time, the Oliveto Citra events do look impressive in light of the positive and negative criteria set down by the Holy See for judging apparitions. Although a definitive official judgment about Oliveto Citra would be premature, individual persons are free to believe or not to believe in the authenticity of the apparitions there. We are free to suspend our personal judgment, or to believe partly in the truth of the Oliveto Citra apparitions, or to believe in the authenticity of some but not of others. We are, moreover, free to accept completely that Our Lady has come to Oliveto Citra, that she appears and speaks there regularly, and that this fact has an important meaning for all of us and for the whole world.

CHAPTER 10

THE MEANING OF OLIVETO CITRA

What do the apparitions at Oliveto Citra mean for the Church? For all mankind? What do they mean for you and for me?

Mary as Mother

Mary appears at Oliveto Citra especially as mother. Frequently she appears with the Infant Jesus in her arms. Besides that, her manner and what she says bring out strongly her maternity with regard to everyone, her motherhood of all. Mary comes to the castle gate as the mother of Jesus and as the mother of each one of us.

Her motherhood of each person, and of all, has a certain intense, urgent, almost fierce quality. There is something almost extreme, excessive, in the number of apparitions, in the number of people to whom Mary appears, in the various signs, such as the frequently smelled perfume and the signs in the sky. This near-excess connotes urgency, intensity, willingness to go to extremes to help, to mother. Mary presents herself as an intensely caring mother, and as a mother who loves not only all, but each one individually.

Mary at Oliveto appears to individual persons. She sometimes calls them by name. She comes to each one a little differently, treats each one differently. Those who see the Blessed Virgin Mary represent all of us, each of us. They stand for us. We can identify with them. Marco and Sabrina De Bellis, Umberto Gagliardi, Antonella Giordano, Tarcisio Di Biasi, Mafalda Caputo, the twins Dino and Carmine Acquaviva, Anita Rio — what they have said to us shows that each has an individual, personal relationship with Mary as mother, each one feels loved by Mary in a special way. What is true for each of them is true for each of us. Each of us has a personal and special relationship with the mother of Jesus as our mother; she loves each of us specially.

And she prays for us, for all mankind and for each one, caring about and for each one, interceding with God — like the mother she is — for each one of us. She intercedes for the world and for every person.

Because she is our mother who loves us and cares for us and prays for us, we can turn to her. She will help us, will guide us, will carry our prayers to God, will lead us to her Son Jesus.

A Call to Prayer, Penance, Conversion

The events at Oliveto Citra have a marked apocalyptic quality. Both in style and in content, the apparitions there have notable apocalyptic aspects. Apocalyptic is a style. It can be a style of writing, as in the New Testament Book of the Apocalypse. Or it can be the style of a situation, of a series of events, as at Oliveto Citra.

The apocalyptic style is characterized by an emphasis on secrets, on hidden things, on the mysterious, and by a stress on divine judgment, on chastisement for sins, on the catastrophic consequences of sinfulness. These factors have their place in the Oliveto Citra apparitions. They give those apparitions, in general, an apocalyptic quality.

The apocalyptic message is a message of hope. Partly because of the apocalyptic aspects, the message of Our Lady at Oliveto Citra is one of hope. God is the Lord of history. History belongs to the Lord. Jesus is victorious over all the forces of evil. And he sends us his mother to call us again to help him, by penance and especially by prayer.

The apocalyptic style and message always contain a prophetic element. In the Old Testament, and also in the New Testament, the prophets call the people to conversion and to greater fidelity to God. Our Lady at Oliveto Citra has a prophetic role in that she speaks to us God's call to conversion, to prayer, and to penance.

Our Lady call us most strongly and most repeatedly to pray, and especially to pray the rosary.

Prayer

We would like to conclude this last chapter with a prayer that Our Lady dictated to Sabrina DeBellis on February 8, 1986.

Mother in heaven, have mercy on us. We love you and we offer ourselves to you. Protect us from evil. Take care of us, Mother in heaven, and help us in all our problems. Mary Queen of the Castle, lead us to heaven. Amen.

APPENDIX

THE ROSARY

The main prayer of the group of pilgrims and residents of Oliveto Citra who meet every evening at the gate to the old castle is the rosary. At about five in the afternoon, and again about eight at night, the crowd in the little square prays all fifteen mysteries of the rosary. It seems appropriate, then, in a book on the Oliveto Citra apparitions, to add an appendix on the rosary.

The Fifteen Mysteries

The rosary is a biblical prayer that uses mainly prayers from the New Testament — the "Our Father" and the "Hail Mary" — and that considers scenes from the Gospel accounts of Jesus' life, death, resurrection, and post-resurrection life. Each "Our Father" and every ten "Hail Mary's" is called a "decade." The entire rosary has fifteen decades. Each decade is dedicated to a mystery of the life of Jesus Christ. The first five decades, or mysteries, take up the earthly life of Jesus; they are called the "Joyful Mysteries." The second five are about his passion and death; these are the "Sorrowful Mysteries." The last five mysteries, the "Glorious Mysteries," consider Jesus' resurrection and the events after that.

Here are the fifteen mysteries of the rosary.

The Joyful Mysteries:

1. The Annunciation: The angel Gabriel announces to Mary that she will be the mother of the Savior, and Mary accepts (Luke 1:26-28).

2. The Visitation: Mary visits her cousin Elizabeth who is pregnant with John the Baptist (Luke 1:39-56).

3. The Nativity: Jesus is born (Luke 2:1-20).

4. The Presentation: Mary and Joseph present Jesus to God in the temple (Luke 2:21-39).

5. The Finding in the Temple: Mary and Joseph find Jesus in the temple sitting among the teachers (Luke 2:41-51).

The Sorrowful Mysteries:

1. The Agony in the Garden: Jesus suffers agony, even to sweating blood, in the Garden of Gethsemane (Luke 22:39-46).

2. The Scourging at the Pillar: Jesus is beaten with whips (Mark 15:15; Matthew 27:26).

3. Jesus is Crowned with Thorns: Jesus is made fun of and a crown of thorns is placed on his head (Matthew 27:28-29).

4. Jesus carries His Cross: Jesus takes up his cross and carries it to the hill of Golgotha (Luke 23:26).

5. Jesus is Crucified: Jesus is nailed to the cross and so dies (Luke 23:33-41).

The Glorious Mysteries:

1. The Resurrection: Jesus rises from the dead (John 20).

2. The Ascension: Jesus ascends to the right hand of the Father (Mark 16:19; Acts 1:9-11).

3. The Holy Spirit comes upon the Apostles at Pentecost: The disciples, together with Mary, gathered in the upper room, receive the outpouring of the Holy Spirit (Acts 2).
4. The Assumption: Jesus takes the body of his mother into heaven where it is reunited with her soul.
5. Mary is Crowned Queen of Heaven: Jesus crowns his mother as the Queen of Heaven.

How to Say the Rosary

Each decade of the rosary is said in the following way:

One ''Our Father'':

Our Father who art in heaven,
Hallowed be thy name.
Thy Kingdom come.
Thy will be done,
On earth as it is in heaven.
Give us today our daily bread;
And forgive us our trespasses,
As we forgive those who trespass against us;
And lead us not into temptation,
But deliver us from evil.
Amen.

Ten ''Hail Mary's'':

Hail Mary, full of grace,
the Lord is with thee.
Blessed art thou among women,
And blessed is the fruit of thy womb,
Jesus.
Holy Mary, Mother of God,
Pray for us sinners
now, and at the hour of our death.
Amen.

One ''Glory Be'':

Glory be to the Father
and to the Son
and to the Holy Spirit.
As it was in the beginning,
is now,
and ever shall be
world without end.
Amen.

These prayers are said for each of the fifteen decades. Each mystery is announced at the beginning of the decade, before the "Our Father."

A common way to pray the rosary is not to think about the words of the prayers, not to dwell on the words you are saying. Rather, you can simply look at a mental picture of the mystery of that particular decade. For example, for the first decade of the Joyful Mysteries, you can have a picture in your imagination of the angel announcing the good news to Mary. Or, instead of a mental picture, the idea of the Annunciation to Mary, or perhaps just looking at Mary or at Jesus or at God with the eyes of faith. In this way, the rosary becomes a kind of contemplative prayer, a looking in faith.

It is customary to say the five Joyful Mysteries on Mondays and Thursdays, the five Sorrowful Mysteries on Tuesdays and Fridays, and the five Glorious Mysteries on Wednesday, Saturdays, and Sundays. However, many people today say all fifteen mysteries every day.

In some places, the Apostles' Creed is said at the beginning of the rosary, followed sometimes by an "Our Father," three "Hail Mary's", and a "Glory Be." This is not the practice at Oliveto Citra; the rosary begins with the "Our Father" of the first decade.

The Litany of Our Lady

Sometimes, as at Oliveto Citra, the Litany of Our Lady, also called the Litany of Loreto, is recited after the fifteen decades of the rosary. An additional invocation is added, "Queen of the Castle, pray for us," near the end of the Litany. Here is the Litany:

Lord, have mercy on us.
Christ, have mercy on us.
Lord, have mercy on us.
Christ, hear us.
Christ, graciously hear us.

God the Father of heaven,	have mercy on us.
God the Son, Redeemer of the world,	have mercy on us.
God the Holy Spirit,	have mercy on us.
Holy Trinity, one God,	have mercy on us.
Holy Mary,	pray for us.
Holy Mother of God,	pray for us.
Holy Virgin of virgins,	pray for us.
Mother of Christ,	pray for us.
Mother of the Church,	pray for us.
Mother of divine grace,	pray for us.
Mother most pure,	pray for us.
Mother most chaste,	pray for us.
Mother inviolate,	pray for us.
Mother undefiled,	pray for us.
Mother most amiable,	pray for us.
Mother most admirable,	pray for us.
Mother of good counsel,	pray for us.
Mother of our Creator,	pray for us.
Mother of our Savior,	pray for us.
Virgin most prudent,	pray for us.
Virgin most venerable,	pray for us.
Virgin most renowned,	pray for us.
Virgin most powerful,	pray for us.
Virgin most merciful,	pray for us.
Virgin most faithful,	pray for us.
Mirror of justice,	pray for us.
Seat of wisdom,	pray for us.

Cause of our joy,	pray for us.
Spiritual vessel,	pray for us.
Vessel of honor,	pray for us.
Singular vessel of devotion,	pray for us.
Mystical rose,	pray for us.
Tower of David,	pray for us.
Tower of ivory,	pray for us.
House of gold,	pray for us.
Ark of the covenant,	pray for us.
Gate of Heaven,	pray for us.
Morning star,	pray for us.
Health of the sick,	pray for us.
Refuge of sinners,	pray for us.
Comforter of the afflicted,	pray for us.
Help of Christians,	pray for us.
Queen of Angels,	pray for us.
Queen of Patriarchs,	pray for us.
Queen of Prophets,	pray for us.
Queen of Apostles,	pray for us.
Queen of Martyrs,	pray for us.
Queen of Confessors,	pray for us.
Queen of Virgins,	pray for us.
Queen of all Saints,	pray for us.
Queen conceived without original sin,	pray for us.
Queen assumed into heaven,	pray for us.
Queen of the most holy Rosary,	pray for us.
Queen of peace,	pray for us.
Queen of the Castle,	pray for us.
Lamb of God, you take away the sins of the world,	spare us, O Lord.
Lamb of God, you take away the sins of the world,	graciously hear us, O Lord.
Lamb of God, you take away the sins of the world,	have mercy on us.

V Pray for us, O holy Mother of God,
R That we may be made worthy of the promises of Christ. Let us pray.

Grant your servants continual health of mind and body, O Lord God. Let the intercession of the blessed ever-virgin Mary gain for us freedom from our present sorrow. Give us the joy of everlasting happiness. Through Christ our Lord. Amen.